Traditions:

Integrating the Days of Awe and Chanukah into the Waldorf Grades Curriculum

Traditions

Integrating the Days of Awe and
Chanukah
into the Waldorf Grades Curriculum

by

Erica Jayasuriya

Printed with support from the Waldorf Curriculum Fund

Published by:
The Association of Waldorf Schools
of North America
Publications Office
65–2 Fern Hill Road
Ghent, NY 12075

Title: *Traditions:*
    Integrating the Days of Awe and Chanukah into the
    Waldorf Grades Curriculum
Author: Erica Jayasuriya
Editor: David Mitchell
Cover: Hallie Wootan
Cover Painting: *Blue Violinist* by Marc Chagall
Proofreader: Ann Erwin
ISBN # 978-1-888365-77-1
© 2008 by AWSNA Publications and Erica Jayasuriya
All copyrights secured by the author

Table of Contents

Acknowledgements 7

Preface 9

Introduction 15

Midrash in the Jewish Tradition 19

The Days of Awe: Rosh Hashanah and Yom Kippur 21

Symbols and Traditions of the Days of Awe 27
    Rosh Hashanah and Yom Kippur in the First Grade 31
    Rosh Hashanah and Yom Kippur in the Second Grade .. 37
    Rosh Hashanah and Yom Kippur in the Third Grade 45
    Rosh Hashanah and Yom Kippur in the Fourth Grade .. 58
    Rosh Hashanah and Yom Kippur in the Fifth Grade 67
    Rosh Hashanah and Yom Kippur in the Sixth Grade 70
    Rosh Hashanah and Yom Kippur in the Seventh Grade 76
    Rosh Hashanah and Yom Kippur in the Eighth Grade 79

Chanukah 97

Symbols and Traditions of Chanukah 105
    Chanukah in the First Grade 109
    Chanukah in the Second Grade 119
    Chanukah in the Third Grade 129
    Chanukah in the Fourth Grade 137
    Chanukah in the Fifth Grade 146
    Chanukah in the Sixth Grade 164
    Chanukah in the Seventh Grade 177
    Chanukah in the Eighth Grade 185

Conclusion 209

Appendix 1 – High Holiday and Chanukah Dates 212

Appendix 2 – Selected Sources for Jewish Books
 and Judaica 213

Appendix 3 – Permissions 214

Endnotes 217

Bibliography 222

Acknowledgements

In many ways this book came about through the impulses and inspirations found in the various communities through which I have traveled. While at Antioch I received the guidance and encouragement of Torin Finser, who was my mentor and thesis advisor while writing this for Antioch and to whom I am deeply grateful. Wade Whistler was a fellow student who was the first of many copy editors.

At Portland Waldorf School I was encouraged by the whole community but wish to give particular credit to Dolores Julian, Virginia Berg, Francine Adams, and Nancy Pierce, all of whom were willing to try out the curriculum with their students and gave me feedback on what worked and what needed revision.

For help in deepening my understanding of Judaism and how to best bridge the worlds of Waldorf and Judaism, I am indebted to Rabbi Michael Tayvah and his wife Paola, both of whom became not only guides but also friends. I received additional help with women's Judaica from Marcia Cohen Spiegel. Ray Pollicker welcomed me into his home and shared his Sephardic family traditions.

At Cedarwood School I have been blessed to work with a wonderful group of colleagues. I am particularly grateful to Mary Jo AbiNader for her new ideas and to Shannon Foby for her feedback on the music curriculum.

I am grateful to David Mitchell at AWSNA not only for being interested in my work, but for being patient with me in the intervening years between our initial plans and final publication. Jessica Orsini, a student at Reed, helped me with copyright research, and Mont Christopher Hubbard, also a Reedie, truly saved me with his knowledge of Finale.

Finally, this book could never have been written without the love and support of my family. My mother, Janet Carnay, acted as a copy editor, Judaica researcher, and asker-of-all-the-right-questions to keep me going deeper into the relationships between the pedagogy and the spirit. Kahlil, Ron, Jill and Isaiah, I thank you for your support and the gift of time that you allowed me to take to bring this work to fruition. I am truly blessed.

Preface

This project began in September of 1995 during my second grade internship at the Portland Waldorf School. At one point during a faculty meeting, the teachers found themselves in a conundrum. The parent body had many Jewish families who were voicing concern over the cycle of festivals in the Waldorf school. The faculty all agreed that they would like to better represent the Jewish families in the celebrations of the school. However, none of the teachers felt familiar enough with the Jewish festivals to guide the school in a proper direction. They also did not want to turn the teaching of these festivals over to parents who did not have a background in anthroposophy. It was at this juncture that I offered my services to the school as both a Jewish woman and a Waldorf teacher.

Throughout the four months I was at the school I pieced together some poems and stories for the faculty. Yet I grew increasingly aware of how minimal my contributions were in light of all the Judaica available to me. Given enough time to sort through vast amounts of stories and poems, I believed a curriculum could be created that would address the needs of both the teachers and the families. While working in the classroom it became clear to me that the background research would need to come later, and that during my internship I needed to engage in "action research."

I was very fortunate to have a co-operating teacher who has devoted herself to the mission of the festivals in the Waldorf schools. Dolores Julian quickly became my mentor and friend, and through almost daily conversations she helped me to deepen my understanding of the festivals. I was also very fortunate to work with her during her second grade year when she introduced the saints stories to the children. Her approach to the saints created a foundation upon which the seasonal festival life of the school was enlivened for children. My research at the time was purely observational. I monitored how the children responded to the stories and how they then reacted to the festivals. It became clear that the festivals were not abstract celebrations for these second graders because they had already developed a relationship to Saint George, Saint Martin, Santa Lucia, and Saint Nicholas through the stories and drawings done in main lesson.

Through discussions with teachers at both the Antioch Summer program and the Portland school, I heard many Waldorf teachers considering eliminating some of the stories of the saints and replacing them with more multi-cultural stories. My observations of that second grade class made it clear that the saints stories are undoubtedly the true framework upon which all of the school festival life is built. The saints stories create a common festival language in the classroom that goes beyond differences in religious identity. The second grade teacher, in penetrating these stories, becomes a guide for both the children and, perhaps more importantly, the parents, as to the reason why the school celebrates these festivals annually.

I contrasted the second grade experience with that of the older children in the school. Some of the other classes had not been as deeply submerged in the saints stories while in second grade, and I wanted to observe how they responded to the festivals. I began by watching the classes during festival assemblies. Of course, I had to take into account that some irreverent behavior is age appropriate, especially in the middle school. I noticed that the classes whose teachers were engaged in festival study and were interested in penetrating their significance on a personal and spiritual level, appeared more attentive and participatory. The classes with teachers who were less engaged in the festival life of the school were more fidgety, their attention blatantly scattered. I also noticed that classes that brought a festival poem or song, rather than something unrelated to the season, exhibited more signs of ownership of the festival.

Those children were quicker to hush children who were being disruptive while others performed. They also appeared to stand more erect and spoke more audibly when it was their turn in assembly.

That year the school decided to have a Chanukah assembly that was separate from the Advent/Christmas assembly. I supplied some poems and songs that I had gathered quickly. Because we organized the Chanukah assembly at the last minute, many of the classes had only one or two days to learn their pieces. It became obvious to me that we were engaging in pure tokenism. The teachers had been unable to help the children develop an adequate relationship to Chanukah, and this was reflected in their presentations, which lacked both enthusiasm and integrity. Having witnessed other festival assemblies, I knew that both the teachers and the children could do much better.

In the school's defense, they did the best they could with very little preparation. In the discussion of the assembly at the following faculty meeting, the need for expanded research became even clearer. If we want to honor other cultural festivals in a way that is meaningful to everyone, the teachers need more background information on the holidays, as well as more practical resources, that will help enable them to make a true inner connection to what they are bringing to the class. A well-informed teacher can provide for the children an experience of the festivals that is full of life. My ideal was to create a Jewish holiday curriculum that would be resonant with the teacher's approach and that would activate thinking, feeling and willing in its lessons.

The need for a teaching guide also became evident when I observed various families bringing the holidays into the classrooms. I firmly believe that there ought to be opportunities for parents to bring in treats and traditions to share with the class. However, my observations showed a tendency in parents to go beyond the sharing of the blessings, food and songs. They also tried to explain the holiday to the children and in doing this, ended up giving abstract concepts to the children rather than providing them the picture-consciousness that is at the very heart of Waldorf education in the elementary grades. This concept-oriented approach only further isolated the children from the true nature of the festivals. I observed a great deal of frustration in the teachers who were aware of this schism. Because they were completely reliant on the parents, the teachers had to assume a gesture of willingness to take the good with the bad, unable to find a way to guide the parents or take over the presentation themselves. These observations led me to present the Jewish festival curriculum in a way that allows the teacher to either lead all of the activities or offer the guide to the parents as a model upon which they can base their presentations.

When I finished my internship at the Portland Waldorf School, the period of "action research" ended. I began a long period of literature review which I divided into four parts: anthroposophic writings on the festivals, history of the Jewish holidays, Rudolf Steiner's pedagogical indications, and poems and folktales of the Jewish people. Since I was more familiar with the Jewish festivals than the anthroposophic festivals, I decided to first deepen my understanding of Steiner's indications for the festivals through a study of anthroposophic literature. This gave me the foundation I needed to compare and contrast the festivals. I was interested primarily in the relationships between the festivals that occur at the same point in the yearly cycle. While my research was focused on Michaelmas and Advent, I also reviewed the other festivals of the year in order to form a more complete picture of the cycle.

Once I had a base in anthroposophy, I began reading the histories of the Jewish holidays. I found many books that offered symbolic pictures of the holidays. I carried these pictures with me and began to let them intermingle with the pictures that had arisen from my anthroposophical readings. As the relationships between the festivals became clearer, I became more and more excited about my research. I was finding connections that I knew would help teachers bring the material to the students in ways that would be personally, and professionally, relevant.

The next step was to gather as much literature on the Jewish holidays as I could find. I reviewed children's books, books for adults, anthologies of poems and anthologies of stories. I also explored Jewish educational materials, hoping they would already contain ideas for lessons that would also work in this context. There was no one definitive source where I found these materials. However, I am profoundly indebted to the anthologies compiled by Philip Goodman and highly recommend his books for additional poems, stories, songs, games, and even dances, should the teacher seek more material. Reading through the literature was the longest part of this process. For every story I found that worked with the indications Steiner gave for the grades, there were dozens that did not.

As I began organizing stories and verses, I noticed that some parts of the curriculum were more coherent than others. I realized that I needed to deepen my understanding of some aspects of the pedagogy, so I re-read many parts of Steiner's books on pedagogy and child development. When, after reading, I still was unsure how to continue, I thought about the children at the school. I found that when I moved out of the abstract thought of "sixth grade" into a consideration of the needs of specific sixth graders, I could begin to fill in the gaps. The writing of the curriculum came together only when I combined the background in anthroposophy, the history and traditions of the Jewish festivals, the pedagogical indications, the folk tales and poems of the Jewish people and, most of all, a picture of the real people in the school whom this project would serve.

The more I worked on this project, the more interest it generated within our community. When I told people what I was working on, they always expressed enthusiasm. The Jewish families, the non-Jewish families, and the faculty were all equally supportive. The general reaction to my undertaking was: "We really need something like this." Nevertheless, some Jewish families, while excited about my work, remained skeptical as to whether the Waldorf school would actually implement any of my suggestions. This attitude influenced an important part of my methodology, which was to make implementation both easy and familiar.

With this project I have sought to unite certain aspects of the Jewish festival experience with the festival life and rhythm of the Waldorf school. Ultimately both anthroposophy and Judaism share profound spiritual truths arising from the pictures offered by the festivals. I am particularly grateful to Rabbi Michael Tayvah and his wife Paola, who earnestly helped me navigate the two worlds of Waldorf and Judaism. Their input and reflections were essential in getting this work to a deeper level.

Ten years have passed since I wrote this guide originally. Since then I have worked in many capacities in the Waldorf schools in Portland: early childhood teacher, grades teacher, consultant, Core Chair. I have worked with hundreds of parents from so many different backgrounds and I have been moved by the common dream to educate our children in a manner different from the norm. I have yet to meet even one family that, in coming to Waldorf education, has not had to find a way of embracing that which is unfamiliar and sometimes uncomfortable. I hope that this guide helps schools to reach back out into the community with a similar gesture. I have tried to create an opportunity for both the teacher and the children to experience reverence for different traditions and history. My hope is that my work will be put to practical use so that the children, families and teachers will continue to discover a common ground amongst peoples and traditions.

This has been an exciting ongoing research experience, and I hope it may serve as a model for other people who wish to be more fully represented in the Waldorf schools. When we take the time to honor the biographies within our community, then the Waldorf school becomes a powerful healing social organism and the lives of our children richer.

– Erica Jayasuriya
January 2008

Introduction

I am beginning to understand that multiculturalism is one of the richest and most complex issues we have undertaken as Waldorf educators.[1]

In AWSNA Publication's booklet *Multiculturalism in Waldorf Education,* Joan Almon addresses the need for Waldorf schools to better represent the cultural backgrounds of the families who have found their way to Waldorf education. She speaks of the need to include non-European stories and suggests finding stories from "Africa, Asia, Latin America, [and] Native American life."[2] Yet in many schools the largest minority of children are not the ones who are mentioned in the above list. The focus on non-European people as the next step in the creation of a multicultural curriculum potentially dismisses the needs of Jewish children and their families already committed to Waldorf education.

The Jewish experience in America is decidedly different from that of other minorities. When the day-to-day gives way to festival seasons, many North American African-Americans, Asians, and Latinos are united with European culture through their common religious bonds, while the Jewish community stands separated from the prevailing cultural norms.

The rhythm of the Waldorf school is connected to the cycle of the year and the celebration of the Christian festivals. The intention of these festivals is to bring the community together and help instill in the children a sense of reverence. Unfortunately, festival life can occasionally turn into an area of contention, rather than unification, in many schools throughout North America. Even among parents with Christian backgrounds, the festivals celebrated school-wide in a Waldorf school sometimes feel foreign and somewhat odd. It cannot be stressed enough that educating all parents about the festivals should be a primary goal if the school wishes the community to embrace the yearly cycle of its social life.

More and more Jewish families are choosing to give their children a Waldorf education. As members of the school community, they are requesting that schools re-examine the purpose of the festival celebrations and how they are brought to the children. Waldorf education strives to bring harmony to the young child, but this can be undermined if the festivals create a sense of isolation and discord in the souls of the children.

One solution is to expand the festival celebrations so that some parts of the Jewish holidays are included. This should be done not as a token gesture, but with the same depth that penetrates all aspects of teaching in Waldorf schools. The question I have set out to "answer" is how to bring the Jewish festivals to the children in a way that is harmonious with both Steiner's pedagogy and Jewish tradition.

What follows is a guide for teachers for the major Jewish holidays that occur in the fall and winter: Rosh Hashanah, Yom Kippur, and Chanukah. The first part of the school year is typically filled with celebrations of Michaelmas, Martinmas, Santa Lucia, Saint Nicholas, and Advent, and thus is weighted toward a strong Euro-Christian perspective. I have found that the festival life of the school significantly abates during the late winter and spring, and the issues of inclusion are not as "hot" during that part of the year. However, it should be noted that the Jewish festival of Passover usually falls close to Easter. Some schools have taken to extending their spring break to make sure that Passover is also included in the break time, as it is perhaps the most family-centric Jewish holiday and requires much physical preparation. In my research I have come to see the threefold nature of these main Jewish holidays. The Days of Awe represent the feeling life, Chanukah represents the thinking life, and Passover, in story and deed, is truly a representation of the willing life. While it is not as necessary, in my opinion, for the entire school to celebrate Passover every year, I would sincerely hope that each third grade has an opportunity to experience the Passover Seder as a manifestation of will.

The busy-ness of the festival season can often overwhelm teachers, and I am sure that the idea of including "one more thing" might appear daunting at first. To best help the teacher, I have tried to create an opportunity for these holidays to be shared in a natural and integrative way within each classroom by focusing on poems and songs that can be included in morning circle work, and with stories that can be told either as part of main lesson, as part of an extra main, or even during snack or lunch time. For each festival I have included circle verses, stories, and poetry that complement the indicated Waldorf curriculum for each grade. At the end of each section are holiday songs that the children can sing or play on their instruments. In cases where copyright permission was unobtainable, I have listed the title, source and brief explanation of the recommended material, which should be available through local libraries and bookstores. It is my hope that by using this guide, teachers will discover that it is indeed possible to integrate the Jewish festivals into the Waldorf curriculum while remaining true to the indications for Waldorf teaching.

Just as the Waldorf curriculum builds upon each preceding year, the curriculum also maintains a continuum. To help the teachers of upper grades better orient themselves, I recommend taking the time to look over the whole curriculum guide. For each of the holidays presented I have included a general overview of the holiday including historical background, modern thoughts on the holiday, how it relates to anthroposophy, and ways that the holiday speaks to the experience of teaching. There is a brief overview of the symbols and traditions that are part of the celebrations, as well as the customary prayers and blessings. Each holiday is then divided by grade starting with first grade and continuing up through eighth grade. The introduction to each grade provides a general overview of how the stories and verses relate to the specific curriculum and developmental indications of that grade. The teacher may choose to read only these introductions or may prefer reading through the stories and verses. While each selection has been carefully chosen for its relationship to the corresponding grade, the teacher who is just beginning to introduce the Jewish festivals may want to incorporate some of the verses and songs from the earlier grades.

There has been much discussion over gender bias in scholarly writing. Rather than alternate he and she, I have chosen to use the pronoun she when referring to the teacher. While it is not my intention to discriminate against the men in this field, the vast majority of Waldorf teachers are women. Think of the words "she" and "her" not as gender specific but as representations of the "feminine" principles of nurturing and compassion, which engender all those who enter into the service of teaching.

This has been an exciting exploration, and I hope that it will help to bring even more harmony to the beauty of the fall and winter festival season in Waldorf schools.

Midrash in the Jewish Tradition

Imagine sitting at a large, round wooden table with a group of wise, elder women as they read text from the Hebrew Bible, or *Torah*. Perhaps the text is the story of Exodus. After reading a passage that includes a brief mention of Miriam, Moses' sister, the women pause and reflect. Then the women begin to ask questions: "How old do you think she is? What is the youngest she could be? What is the oldest she could be? Whose idea is it to hide the baby? Why is she later referred to as a prophetess? What is a prophetess? What do they do? Why is her song the first song in the Torah? How would you compare Miriam to other girls and women in the Torah?"[3]

The energy in the room changes. Discussion and reflection inspire imaginations, and the women begin to tell stories, write poems, and compose music to further embody the story of Miriam. This process is a modern form of an ancient Jewish tradition called *midrash*, a Hebrew word literally meaning "to draw out."[4] Traditionally it was done by rabbis and scholars who would study the Torah and then parlay their discussions into metaphors, legends, and parables that would speak to their congregants.[5] (This collection of rabbinic discussions regarding laws, customs, and ethics is called the *Talmud*.) The Jewish tradition greatly values the role of story, poetry and music as a means to further deepen one's relationship with the Torah and God.

As time moved on, the activity of midrash was also used to help make sense not only of the Torah, but also of the historic events that greatly affected the Jewish people. In many ways Steiner's words, "Imbue thyself with the power of imagination, have courage for the truth, sharpen thy feeling for responsibility of soul,"[6] speak directly to the essence of the Jewish people and culture. By continually imbuing themselves in the power of imagination, rabbis, scholars, and artists throughout time have helped inspire the Jewish community to become active and engaged world citizens.

The material included in this curriculum arises mostly out of this tradition. Hopefully the stories will work for you and your students. However, if after reading something, you feel that there are parts that speak to you and others that do not, do not be afraid to change things to suit your class. You may at first approach this intellectually, but remember to allow yourself to be inspired! Welcome your imaginations and know that by doing so you are creating a bridge between Judaism and anthroposophy. The power of imagination is the path to freedom.

The Days of Awe: Rosh Hashanah and Yom Kippur

For children the year begins anew in September. At that time, as summer fades away, there is a palpable feeling of preparation for school. Children get new clothes, new notebooks and pencils, even new haircuts. Sometimes a new teacher and new classmates greet them on the first day of school. Clearly, the children's experience of the cycle of the year is deeply connected to fall as a time of renewal. They do not experience nearly as much newness during the dark days of winter. For instance, they cannot relate to the ritually vacant, all-night long celebration that marks the change of the calendar year for adults. If you ask teachers which feels more like the beginning of a new year, September or January, more often than not September is the answer. The question remains then: How can we acknowledge a sense of new beginnings in the fall when most of the culture around us waits until January to celebrate?

It is fortuitous for the teacher who wants to include the Jewish holidays in her curriculum that *Rosh Hashanah*, the Jewish New Year, almost always falls in conjunction with the first or second week of the school year.[7] The teacher can use Rosh Hashanah as a vehicle for celebrating the beginning of a new cycle with her class. The traditions of Rosh Hashanah can also serve as a tool for reflecting upon the past year as a class and as individuals.

In Judaism, the month before *Tishri*, when the new year begins, is called *Elul*. Elul is traditionally experienced as a time of deep reflection, study, and daily meditations on the past year. Because of these meditations, every day of Elul is infused with an inner preparation for the coming year. Elul is thirty days long and Rosh Hashanah falls on the tenth day of Tishri, so we see here the significance of a forty-day transition period before awakening to something new.[8] The work of Elul is like a lemniscate. There is a continuum of looking forward and looking back.

This is not unlike the way a teacher prepares for the new school year. She must reflect upon the previous year(s) in order to shape the one to come. Because Elul is a time for active reflection, it is also the time when God's "word" can best be heard. This is another way in which the work of Elul, which is usually in August, is similar in nature to the inner work that a Waldorf teacher undertakes around the same time. Ideally, by mid-August most of the curriculum materials have been gathered and the teacher can then open herself up to guidance and inspiration from the spiritual world. Now we begin to see that, while a Waldorf teacher initially may feel that the Jewish holiday experience is totally foreign, it is, in fact, quite familiar.

It is important to note that Rosh Hashanah, the "new year of years and creation," is not the only new year's holiday in the Jewish calendar. Another new year begins in the month of *Nisan* (March or April) and is marked by the celebration of Passover. Thus a new year also begins in spring and correlates to the beginning of the history of the Jews as free people. Rosh Hashanah marks the changing of year, while Passover marks the changing of months. Rosh Hashanah is the beginning of the seventh month of the Hebrew calendar, so it is the Sabbath month. It demands that we take time out to rest and reflect, just as God did on the seventh day. Rosh Hashanah is a celebration of Genesis and is a time to acknowledge the birthday of the world and the magnificence of all its creatures.

Rosh Hashanah literally means "head of the year," head being the image of our heads raised towards heaven. There is a lot of heavenly imagery during Rosh Hashanah and *Yom Kippur*, more than in any of the other Jewish festivals. This is why they are often referred to as high holy days or, preferably, the "Days of Awe." The awesome-ness comes from the experience of looking deeply into the human condition and then towards God. This experience for Jews is like a first grader's experience on the first day of school, when their teacher seems so big and all-knowing. Within the awe there is an incredible desire to do right and strive to become one's best.

The work of intense inner preparation during Elul is based on the understanding that on *Erev* Rosh Hashanah,[9] the Book of Life is opened. Jews believe that on Rosh Hashanah all creatures are inscribed either in the Book of Life, in the Book of Death, or in neither. The majority of people fall in the "neither" category, and the ten days between Rosh Hashanah and Yom Kippur are used to tilt the scales in favor of inscription in the Book of Life. Then on Yom Kippur each person's fate is sealed for the year.

It is said that Rosh Hashanah marks the opening of heaven's gates, which remain open until the end of Yom Kippur. During this time, Jews have the opportunity to transcend the daily experiences of Judaism and connect with the higher worlds. While the Gates of Heaven are open, there is an opportunity for deeper communication between the spiritual world and the physical world. The Days of Awe are a time for divine guidance from God but also from those who have departed the physical world. This is why *Yizkor* is an important part of Yom Kippur. Yizkor is the lighting of memorial candles for family and friends and the saying of special prayers for the deceased. These prayers are not about sorrow, but rather about the strength of life. The prayers convey a sense that those remaining on earth will go on living as best they can in honor and remembrance of those who have passed. During these Days of Awe, we are working closely with the spiritual world. For these ten days, the philosophies of Judaism and anthroposophy intermingle.

The joyousness of the new year, as celebrated during Rosh Hashanah, is solemnized at Yom Kippur. Yom Kippur is a time to move even deeper into ourselves by asking forgiveness of those we have harmed or by atoning for when we "missed the mark."[10] Unlike other religions wherein sins are absolved through prayer, Judaism allows only for sins directly against God to be forgiven by Him through prayer. The majority of the prayers on Yom Kippur are filled with encouragement for individuals to go forth and speak with the people in their lives that they may have hurt. Essential to Judaism is the idea *Tikkun O'lam*, or "Repair of the World." In order to carry out this intention, Judaism teaches that we must take direct responsibility for our actions involving others. This is a very profound element of Yom Kippur. It is not simply a matter of remembering our offenses. Yom Kippur demands that we actually act upon these realizations and be willing to forgive others as well.

While the Days of Awe are focused mostly on the feeling life, one also needs to activate the will in order to carry out the requirements of true remorse and forgiveness. One cannot be passive throughout these holy days. This is a time to work less from the impulses of our ego and more from our soul-spirit. The tradition of fasting on Yom Kippur, for instance, is actually symbolic of allowing the body to "decay" so that the soul may be the primary focus of the day.[11] The teachings of forgiveness move from God to fellow man and then finally to our own selves. Ultimately, we must let go of our own guilt and shame and forgive ourselves for our human weaknesses. It is the practice of asking for forgiveness and granting forgiveness that "tips the scales" and allows the Jewish people to be sealed in the Book of Life for a good and sweet New Year.

The Days of Awe, and Yom Kippur in particular, are resonant with the festival of Michaelmas. Steiner indicated that Michael is the angel of the Jewish people, as he is the guide of their collective folk soul. While many practicing Jews today do not have a lot of angel consciousness, classical Jewish life and thought were filled with angelic beings. While it is perhaps coincidental, it is interesting that their most holy days of the year are devoted to the mission of Michael. Rabbi Areyeh Hirschfield has expressed that Yom Kippur is truly about casting off the material world and moving deeper into "nothingness and what is beyond nothingness," which in Jewish mysticism are *Ayin* and *Yod*.[12] In his lectures on Michael, Steiner draws from Faust, saying, "In thy Nothingness I hope to find the All." He concludes that, to take up the mission of Michael, "We must resolve to look into that realm where materialism sees 'Nothingness' and see the spiritual world."[13] This is one way in which Yom Kippur and Michaelmas are quite similar in spirit.

Another relationship between Michaelmas and the Days of Awe can be found in the symbolism of the *shofar*. The shofar is a ram's horn that is blown every day during the month of Elul and then one hundred times on Rosh Hashanah. The shofar's sounds, which resemble wailing, groaning, and crying, are meant to pierce the everyday consciousness of the Jewish people and wake them to the spiritual work at hand. Waking to consciousness is the path of our time. Steiner wrote, "Our time demands that we see things as they are, with all their angles and contours. But precisely because these sharp angles and contours are there, the urge also arises in our souls to close our eyes sleepily to these things. . . . If we wish to follow the Archangel Michael, then we must infuse human souls with clarity and overcome sleepiness."[14] The shofar is symbolic of this same need to awaken to clarity.

The Days of Awe are about our humanity. This festival asks not that we be perfect, but that we open our eyes to our imperfections. As Steiner said, "One should open one's eyes, one's spiritual eyes, to be sure! Once we open our eyes, our will follows. Our will depends upon our life situation. It is not always possible in our particular circumstances to do the right thing according to our karma; but we must try to open our eyes spiritually."[15] We will falter, but it is through remembering our mistakes that we rise and begin anew, wiser still. This is an ideal that transcends religion and can be brought right into the classroom as a tool for learning and living.

Faculty Verse

IN THE DAYS OF AWE

Dangling from a leather sling in the oak,
the tree trimmer, high in the swaying tree,
reaches out to saw away a branch.
It leaves a staring eye when it drops,
a round white eye on the tree trunk.
Cautiously, with rope and saw,
tools swinging from his belt,
he crawls upward, seeking limbs to cut.

Now I too slash away unnecessary branches,
opening eyes to the sky.
Imperiled, dangling, lacking skill to choose
the limbs that stifle growth, I pray
to Thee Whose marks I bear within
like rings of trees.
I pray Thee guide my hand,
I, the tree trimmer, I, the tree.
— Ruth F. Brin[16]

Symbols and Traditions of the Days of Awe

As in all holidays and *Shabbat*, the Jewish Sabbath, the Jewish new year begins with blessings over candles, wine and bread. On Rosh Hashanah, a round loaf to represent the roundness and fullness of the year replaces the traditional braided *challah* bread. A favorite tradition of Rosh Hashanah is the eating of apples dipped in honey. The apples, like the challah, symbolize the new cycle of the year. By dipping the apples in honey we are symbolically coating our year in sweetness. There is a special prayer asking for a good and sweet new year that is recited after the blessing over the apples. Some families have a special ceremonial plate for the apples and honey. A class teacher can have the students make their own plates by decorating regular paper plates and gluing a muffin cup into the center for the honey.

There are other foods that are often part of the Rosh Hashanah celebration. Honey loaf cakes and *Taiglach* candies again symbolize the sweetness of the year. Another favorite dish is *Tzimmes*, a stew of carrots, sweet potatoes and prunes. Some families also eat a baked dish of sliced potatoes and apples, symbolizing man below (potatoes) and heaven above (apples).[17] Recipes for these dishes can be found in many books about the Jewish holidays. Food is an integral part of all Jewish celebrations, and grade school children usually enjoy learning through eating.

During the Days of Awe people wish each other, "*L'Shanah Tovah*," or "Happy new year," though it is customary to translate that as "Good new year," implying that the ups and downs of life make it still good, even if not always happy. In addition people may say, "*Le-Shanah Tovah U-Metukah Tikateyvu*," which means, "May you be inscribed in the book of life." The other person may respond, "*Gam le-mar,*" which means, "The same to you."[18] Many Jewish families send greeting cards at this time of year. Children often enjoy making their own cards and exchanging them with friends and family.

Another important tradition during the Days of Awe is *Tashlikh*, the ritual casting away of transgressions. During morning prayers many psalms are read, including Micah (7:19): "You will cast (Tashlikh) all your sins into the depths of the sea." On the afternoon of the first day of Rosh Hashanah, it is customary to gather at a free-flowing body of water, preferably one with fish, and shake out one's pockets of breadcrumbs and lint into the water. In the book *Seasons of Our Joy*, Arthur Waskow explains, "When we do Tashlikh at the water's edge, we are not trying to get rid of our misdeeds but to transform them. We are trying to seek out and renew the life-giving energy that is concealed within a sin, and turn it into an energy for good. We are trying to give that energy new life, so that it can give new life to us."[19]

Blessings for Rosh Hashanah and Yom Kippur

BLESSING OVER THE CANDLES
>Baruch atah Adonai Eloheynu melech ha'olam asher kid'shanu b'mitzvotav
>V'tzivanu l'hadleek ner shel Yom Tov.
>(On Yom Kippur:)
>V'tzivanu l'hadleek ner shel Yom Ha-Kippurim.
>Blessed is the Eternal our God, Ruler of the universe, who sanctifies us through our commandments and commands us to kindle the New Year (Day of Atonement) Lights.

Alternative translations:
>You are Blessed, Eternal One of Being, our God who is Universal Spirit, Who gives us paths of holiness, like this path of bringing light to this holyday time.[20]
>or
>Blessed are you, Eternal One, Who enables us to welcome Rosh Hashanah by kindling these lights.[21]

BLESSING OVER THE WINE/JUICE
>Baruch atah Adonai Eloheynu melech ha'olam boray p'ree hagafen.
>Blessed is the Eternal our God, Ruler of the universe, Creator of the fruit of the vine.

BLESSING OVER THE BREAD
>Baruch atah Adonai Eloheynu melech ha'olam hamotzi lechem min ha'aretz.
>Blessed is the Eternal our God, Ruler of the universe, who brings forth bread from the earth.

BLESSING OVER THE APPLES AND HONEY
>Baruch atah Adonai Eloheynu melech ha'olam boray p'ri ha'aytz.
>Yehi ratzon milfanecha Adonai Eloheinu v'elohei avoteinu shet'chadesh aleinu shanah tovah um'tukah.
>Blessed is the Eternal our God, Ruler of the universe, who creates the fruits of the tree.

May it be Your will, O Eternal, our God and God of our ancestors, that You renew us for a good and sweet year.

Alternative translation:
> As we eat this fruit of the trees, we pray that the new year will be a sweet and happy one for all of us.[22]

Rosh Hashanah and Yom Kippur in the First Grade

First grade is already filled with awe and wonder. The first grade teacher can behold her students and experience the living spirit of Rosh Hashanah. The children are fresh and ripe for a new beginning. In first grade we can honor that we are beginning not only a new year but also a new cycle, the school cycle of eight years.

The first seven years of life are concerned primarily with the development of the child's will forces. First graders are entering into the next seven-year cycle, which is the period characterized by Steiner as the time when the realm of feeling is developed. The children in the first grade are just crossing over into the realm of feeling. Many may still be six at the beginning of the year when these holidays fall. The first graders can best experience the holidays by focusing exclusively on the pictures and symbols that arise in verses and stories. It would also be ideal if a Jewish family could come into the classroom and share a simple ritual of blessings over bread, apples and juice. The children will delight in dipping apples into honey and can share their verses about the new year with the family. The teacher can talk about the sweetness of the honey and how she hopes that the school year will be a sweet year for the class.

The teacher can work with the symbols of Rosh Hashanah, mainly the shofar, the apples and the round challah, by having the children make these things in beeswax. They are very simple shapes and may not be intimidating to those first graders who have not worked with beeswax before.

The story "Happy Birthday, World!" focuses on Rosh Hashanah as the world's birthday. I believe that this is as much as the first grader really needs to know about Rosh Hashanah. The children could make "birthday" cards for the world as an activity related to the story. Since Rosh Hashanah falls on two consecutive days, the teacher may be able to use the story and activity according to Waldorf pedagogy: tell the story on Erev Rosh Hashanah and make cards the following day after the children have carried it into their sleep. Perhaps the birthday cards can also show what "gift" the child would give to the world. This might offer some insight into the child as well. What is his relationship to the world? Has the incarnating process landed the child on the earth yet, or is the relationship still more ethereal?

It is my sense that the younger children do not need to experience Yom Kippur. Yom Kippur, more than any other Jewish festival, is really a festival for adults and older children. The first grade teacher can best acknowledge Yom Kippur by carrying the images and feelings of forgiveness within her. The six- and seven-year-olds are still working out of imitation, and their teacher's inner striving will touch them all.

Verses for First Grade

Rosh Hashanah 1
>   Mother took some honey
>   And an apple, too.
>   Then she said, "Come here, my child;
>   I have a gift for you.
>   Let's begin the New Year
>   With this little treat.
>   May the year be happy!
>   May the year be sweet!"
>   – Ben Aronin[23]

The Shofar's Sound
>   The shofar's sound is loud and clear.
>   It has a sound I love to hear.
>   A sound that says, "Happy New Year."
>   – Sylvia Rouss[24]

For a Good and a Sweet New Year
>   Bees, bees,
>   Give us your honey!
>   Give us your honey, please.
>   We have special round bread,
>   Apples too, round and red,
>   That came from the orchard trees.
>   We'll eat them with honey,
>   All golden and sunny
>   When Rosh Hashanah is here;
>   Honey, apples, and bread
>   When the blessing is said
>   For a good and a sweet New Year.
>   – Sadie Rose Weilerstein[25]

Happy Birthday, World![26]

by

Sadie Rose Weilerstein

Ruth and Debby were getting ready for a birthday. It wasn't Ruth's birthday or Debby's. It wasn't Danny's birthday or Judith's or Mother's or Daddy's. It wasn't even George Washington's birthday or Abraham Lincoln's. It was the World's birthday. It was Rosh Hashanah, the New Year.

"How old will the world be today?" Ruthie asked Mother.

"Ever so old," said Mother. She was spreading their nicest white cloth on the table and Ruth and Debby were helping her.

"A hundred years old?" asked Ruthie.

"A thousand years old?" asked Debby.

"More than five thousand years old," said Mother.

"There ought to be a birthday cake for the world," said Ruthie, "with candles."

"Goodness," said Mother. "Where could we get a cake big enough? But we'll have our holiday candles and lots and lots of good things. Come and help me put them on the table."

So Ruth and Debby helped. There were two round loaves of challah at Daddy's place. They weren't twisted, like the Sabbath loaves. They were round, for a good round year. And there was honey for a sweet year, and sticky little round honey cakes. There were shiny red apples to dip in the honey. Mm! Ruth and Debby could hardly wait to taste them.

Ruth and Debby danced round and round the table. They were so happy, they made up a little song. Ruth began it:

> "Everything is new on Rosh Hashanah!
> Our shoes are new,
> Our dresses are new,
> Our ribbons are, too.
> Everything is new on Rosh Hashanah
> For a Happy New Year!"

Then Debby sang:

"Everything is round on Rosh Hashanah!
The apples are round,
And the cakes are round,
And the challahs are round and round!
Everything is round on Rosh Hashanah
For a good round year."

"Now it's your turn, Mother," said Ruth and Debby. So Mother sang too:

"Everything is sweet on Rosh Hashanah!
Daddy's flowers are sweet,
And the cakes are sweet,
And the honey is sweet,
And my children are very sweet!
Everything is sweet on Rosh Hashanah
For a good sweet year."

But still Ruth and Debby wished there could be a birthday cake with candles. They didn't say anything about it, because just then Daddy came in from synagogue. Ruth and Debby flew across the room to meet him. "*Le-shanah tovah*! Happy New Year, Daddy," they cried.

After that there were so many things to do. There was Daddy's *Kiddush* (prayer) to listen to. They stood very still and quiet while he thanked God for the New Year. Then Daddy cut one of the big round loaves, and each one dipped a bit of bread in honey.

"*Le-shanah tovah u-metukah*," they said. "For a good sweet year."

They dipped apple in honey, too. Apple is very good when you dip it in honey. Mother's candles blinked brightly, and Daddy sang songs, and it was past their bedtime but they didn't have to go to bed, and the food was so good! But still Ruth and Debby wished there could be a birthday cake with candles.

They told Daddy about it.

"Hmm," Daddy said. "A birthday cake for the world's birthday! Do you know how big it would have to be? If all the wheat fields were one wheat field, and all the scythes were one scythe, and all the mills were one mills; if all the mixing bowls were one mixing bowl, and all the baking pans one baking pan, all the ovens one oven. . . ."

"And all the bowls of frosting one bowl of frosting," Ruthie helped him.

"Of course," said Daddy. "We mustn't forget the frosting. If all the men were one man, one great giant man! If the great giant man took the great big scythe and cut down the great big field of grain; if he ground the grain in the great big mill, and gave the great sack of flour to his great giant wife, and she mixed it in the great big bowl and baked it in the great big pan."

"And frosted it with the great big bowl of frosting," said Ruthie.

"Then maybe," said Daddy, "that great big cake would be big enough to hold the world's birthday candles."

Ruth and Debby laughed. They liked Daddy's stories. But still they wished they could see those candles. "There ought to be birthday candles on a birthday," said Debby.

Then what do you suppose happened? Daddy whispered something to Mother. Mother nodded her head. "Maybe we can find those candles," said Daddy.

The next minute Mother was slipping on Ruth's and Debby's coat and they were all out of doors—out at night, long past their bedtime.

It was very still and shadowy in the garden. "Look up," said Daddy. "Do you see the candles?" Ruth and Debby threw back their heads and raised their eyes to the sky. It was dark and velvety—and it was filled with stars. There were hundreds and hundreds of them, blinking and twinkling like birthday candles.

"The stars are the world's birthday candles," said Debby softly. Her eyes were shining.

Mother and Daddy nodded.

Ruth and Debby looked up at the sky with its twinkling stars and the new moon, the Tishri moon, like a silver cradle. They looked at the grass under their feet, at the elm tree lifting its dark boughs to heaven.

"Happy birthday, world," they said. "Happy New Year!"

Rosh Hashanah and Yom Kippur in the Second Grade

Often in second grade the non-Christian families experience some resistance to the curriculum. Second grade is the time to delve into the essence of the Christian festivals. It is the saints stories that give the children vivid pictures to associate with the festivals celebrated in the Waldorf school. For children who do not already practice these festivals it is even more important to stick to the curriculum and not be swayed away from the saints. Skimping on the second grade curriculum takes away the necessary foundation that non-Christians need in order to avoid feeling alienated by the school festivals. If the child "lives with" Saint Martin for a week in second grade, then she will always reflect on that experience when Martinmas comes around in the yearly cycle. It cannot be stressed enough that the second grade curriculum is a major key to not alienating children and should not be altered if the school intends to follow the traditional festival cycle.

The saints stories speak to what is working in the eight-year-old. Now that they have been in school a year, the children may already be showing signs of hardness towards each other and their environment. Many children in our culture start the "fall" that we associate with the nine-year change already in second grade. The saints stories speak of goodness and kindness towards fellow man and all the creatures of the earth. It is these qualities that are also found in the verses and stories for Rosh Hashanah and Yom Kippur for second graders. More than the sheer festivity that was experienced in first grade, the second grader can begin to hear the messages of charity and forgiveness that are part of the Days of Awe.

Again, a Jewish family could bring the ritual of the blessings, or the teacher can try to speak them for the class. Now that the children are writing, the teacher might want to have the children write out a line in English from the blessings over the apples and honey. It would also be a nice activity if the children wrote New Year's cards saying simply, "*L'Shanah Tovah.*" They could even be sent to one of the Waldorf schools in Israel!

The second grade may enjoy playing the game "Shanah Tovah." In this game the children stand in a circle and one child is the postman. The postman stands in the center and calls out, "I sent a Shanah Tovah card from (Sue) to (Jim)." Those children must then run and change places before the postman tags them. Once a child is caught, he/she becomes the postman.[27]

A different kind of activity that would be appropriate for second graders would be to discuss what is a good deed. They could then share with each other, or the class, a time when they have done a good and kindly deed. Ask the children why they did it and how they felt afterwards. The teacher may choose to notice which children relate deeds involving other children, which talk about adults, which talk about animals, and so forth, as part of the ongoing child study.

Verses for Second Grade

ROSH HASHANAH 2
I dreamed about a great big book
That has your name and mine;
The name of everyone on earth
A name on every line;
And when you do a kindly deed
God writes, "That child is fine!"
— Ben Aronin[28]

ROSH HASHANAH 3
There was a sound so sweet and clear,
It said to me, "The New Year's here."
It said, "Remember to be brave."
It said, "Remember to be good."
And when I heard the shofar's call
I stood up straight and said I would.
— Ben Aronin[29]

Maybe Even Higher[30]

by

I.L. Peretz

Once long ago, in a village where everyone was poor but hopeful, there lived a wise and holy man named Zuzya. Whenever anyone had a worry, the first thing they did was to talk to Zuzya.

Each morning the month before the New Year, the entire village awakened before dawn to say special prayers together. Every person added a few private ones: "Dear God, please let me make enough money to feed my family!" "Please make my mother well!" "Please send my children wonderful marriage partners!" "Stop my neighbor from stealing my chickens!" When the villagers prayed, they were glad Zuzya was there to hear them.

One morning Zuzya was late for praying. The prayer room felt empty without him. "Where could he be?" everyone asked one another. He was nowhere to be seen—not in the prayer house, not in the study house, and not in his own house. The door to his little home stood wide open. Of course, no one would think of stealing from Zuzya.

The villagers agreed that Zuzya could be only in one place—heaven! Every citizen of the town, from the youngest child to the oldest grandmother, needed help. Who else but Zuzya could go to God and ask for help?

Everyone believed this except for one man who was new to the village. He studied day and night, night and day, with his nose nearly touching his book. Behind his back, the villagers called him Stick, because he was dry and lifeless. When he heard Zuzya had gone to heaven to plead for the people, the stranger smiled for the first time in his life. In fact, he fell down laughing at the idea of Zuzya having a chat with God. When he finally stopped laughing, he shrugged and said, "How can you people be so ignorant? Besides, who cares where Zuzya goes in the morning?"

But really, the stranger was curious. Late that night, after evening prayers, he crept into Zuzya's house and crawled under his bed. Zuzya was so absorbed in a conversation with God that he didn't hear the man enter the house. The stranger planned to stay awake the whole night to see where Zuzya went during the early morning prayers.

Somebody else might have fallen asleep, but not a man accustomed to studying day and night, night and day. He read all night under the bed, until he heard a long sigh and a groan over his head. Zuzya had been awake for a while, thinking about the troubles of the people, and his heart hurt for their suffering.

Somebody else might have wept at the sound of Zuzya's sadness, but not the stranger. He was full of learning, not compassion. So he lay there, waiting, without understanding Zuzya's groans.

It was still dark when Zuzya got up. As the springs of the bed creaked, the stranger shivered. Here he was, with the holiest and wisest man in the village, at the holiest time of the day. He began to sweat. His skin became bumpy with goose pimples, but he was a disciplined man. He clenched his jaw to keep his teeth from chattering and didn't budge.

Zuzya went to his closet and took out a bundle. He untied it and pulled out huge boots; baggy, rough pants; a short, clumsy jacket; a big fur hat and a long, broad leather belt studded with brass nail heads. When he put on the clothes, he no longer looked like Zuzya. He looked like a peasant who lived in the forest. From one of the pockets dangled a piece of string. The stranger held his breath as Zuzya knelt beside the bed and pulled out an axe from underneath the mattress. Securing the axe in his belt, Zuzya left the house. The stranger, shaking and sweating, followed.

Zuzya walked quickly along the dark streets, with the moon shining on him between houses. The stranger, close behind him, listened to his thumping heart keeping time to Zuzya's clumping boots.

Zuzya headed for the woods right outside the town, and when he had walked thirty steps, he stopped in front of a young tree. The stranger's mouth dropped open as he saw Zuzya pull the axe from his belt and take a mighty swing at the tree. Two whacks brought it down with a splintery thud. Zuzya quickly lopped off the branches and cut the sapling into kindling. He tied the pieces into a bundle with the string in his pocket, lifted the wood onto his shoulder, poked the axe back into his belt, and turned back toward the village.

Walking down a side street in the poorest neighborhood, he stopped by a tumbledown shack and knocked on a rag-stuffed window.

"Who's there?" asked a weak, frightened voice.

"I!" answered Zuzya roughly, disguising his voice to sound like a woodsman.

"Who's 'I'?" asked the voice within the house.

And Zuzya answered, "Vassil," a common peasant name.

"What do you want, Vassil?"

"I have wood to sell, very cheap," said the make-believe Vassil. And without waiting for permission, he walked into the house.

The stranger crept up to the door and peered in. In the gray light of early morning, he saw a few pieces of broken furniture. In the lopsided bay lay an old woman covered with rags. She struggled to raise her head and said bitterly, "Wood? You expect a poor widow to buy wood? With what?"

"I'll trust you for the money," said the pretend Vassil. "It's only six pennies."

"And how will I ever get six pennies to pay you back?" she whimpered.

"Don't be foolish!" Zuzya said sharply. "You are a poor, sick, old widow, and I am willing to trust you with a little wood—I'm sure you'll pay me back. Yet you don't trust God, the compassionate Source of Life, to give you six miserable cents?"

"And who will light the fire for me?" the old woman groaned. "Have I strength even to lift my head?"

"I'll light the stove for you," Zuzya answered. As Zuzya set the fire, he sang the morning prayers. By the time he said the last prayer, the fire was blazing.

What the stranger witnessed through a crack in the door taught him more than all his books and years of study. From that day on, when Zuzya spoke, the stranger listened.

    Years later, whenever one of the people in the village told their children of the Zuzya who flew straight up to heaven, the stranger never laughed. He only nodded and said softly, "Maybe even higher."

The Tear of Repentance: A Yom Kippur Fantasy[31]

by

Dorothy F. Zeligs

Once upon a time, there was an angel who disobeyed God. The angel was summoned to appear before the throne of judgment to answer for his misdeeds. He pleaded for mercy and begged God to forgive him. God looked down upon the angel kindly and said, "I shall not punish you, but you must atone for your wrongdoing. I will give you a task to perform. Go down to earth and bring to Me the most precious thing in the world."

The angel sped down to earth, happy to have a chance to win God's forgiveness. Over many countries he roamed, for many years, looking for the most precious thing in the world. One day he came upon a great battlefield. He saw a young soldier lying there, badly wounded. This young man had fought bravely in defense of his country and was now dying. The angel caught up the last drop of blood from the soldier's wound and hastened back to heaven with it. "This is indeed a precious thing which you have brought back," God said to the angel. "A soldier who gives his life for his country is very dear to Me. But return, and search once more."

So the angel returned to earth and continued his quest. For many years he roamed, through cities, woods, and plains. Then, one day, he saw a nurse in a great hospital. She was dying of a dread disease. She had nursed others through this illness, working so hard that she had worn down her own strength and so caught the disease herself. She lay pale and gasping upon her cot. As she was dying, the angel caught up her last breath and hastened to heaven with it. "Surely, God," said the angel, "the last breath of this unselfish nurse is the most precious thing in the world."

"It is a very precious thing that you have brought to Me," God replied. "One who gives her life for another is indeed worthy in My sight. But return and search again."

Then the angel returned to earth again to search once more. Far and wide he roamed, for many years. One night, he saw a villainous-looking man on horseback, riding through a dark forest. The man was armed with a sword and a spear. The angel guessed on what wicked errand this man was bound. He was going to avenge himself on the keeper of the forest, who would not permit him to poach the king's game. The man came to the small hut where the forester and his family lived. Light streamed from the window. Getting down from his horse, the villain peered through the window. He saw the wife of the forester putting her little son to bed. He heard her teaching him how to say his evening prayers. Something within his hard heart seemed to melt. Did the scene bring back memories of his own faraway childhood and his own mother, who had taught him to pray? Tears filled the man's eyes and he turned away from his evil deed and repented his ways. The angel caught up one of his tears and flew back to heaven with it.

"This," said God, "is the most precious thing in the world, for it is the tear of someone who is truly sorry. And that is what opens the gates of heaven."

Rosh Hashanah and Yom Kippur in the Third Grade

Just as second grade is a time to breathe in the pictures that make up the Christian festival year, third grade is a time to live into the pictures of the Hebrew people and their festivals. Most third grade teachers begin the year with the creation story from Genesis. When Rosh Hashanah comes around, the children can then understand that the idea of the world's birthday comes from the story of Genesis. Thus, this should be the first time the Genesis story is part of any Rosh Hashanah celebration in the grades. One way to approach this change is to teach the children another name for Rosh Hashanah, *Yom Harat Olam*, which means "The day the world was created."[32]

Now that the children are hearing the stories from the Old Testament, the teacher should review the stories that are read on Rosh Hashanah and Yom Kippur and see if any are appropriate to tell the class this early in the year. On Rosh Hashanah, the story of Sarah and Hagar is told the first day and the binding of Isaac is told the second day. On Yom Kippur the story of Jonah and the Whale is told.[33] If it is too early to tell these stories, I suggest that, when they are eventually told in a later Old Testament block, the teacher mention they are festival stories. The class can then do some recall about the high holidays and look at why those stories would be the ones told year after year during the Days of Awe.

The verse "Yotzer Or" is a traditional part of the holiday liturgy that supports the third grade curriculum of seasons and the calendar. In the spirit of economy in teaching, I suggest that the Jewish date, month and year be written on the board along with the secular version every day of the third grade year. By doing this, the children will become familiar with the lunar calendar and also the Hebrew names of the months. When Rosh Hashanah comes, they will see the changing of the year on the board.

They will experience the new year in a new way because the information will be coming through the eyes rather than through the ears, which is how they experienced it in first and second grade. As part of their calendar study, the teacher can share that the Hebrew calendar has more than one new year! Rosh Hashanah is the new year for years, individual people, and all the creatures of the world. *Tu B'Shevat* is the new year for trees. Passover is the new year for months and the Jewish people becoming a group. The teacher can then ask the children what feels like a new year for them. School starting? A birthday? January first? The first bulbs of spring? In third grade Rosh Hashanah can set the stage for a later calendar block.

There are many activities relating to Rosh Hashanah and Yom Kippur that can complement the practical work studies of third grade. The class can collect apples and make applesauce, which can be used later on Chanukah *latkes*. They can visit a beekeeper to collect a jar of ceremonial honey for Rosh Hashanah. The third grade can also make round challahs and share them with the other classes in the school.

The story "The Announcing Tool" is perfect for third grade because it looks at the need for the shofar to come from the natural world. This story supports the third grade theme of using what the world offers us. An excellent poem for recitation is called "Blowing the Shofar," which can be found in the book *Milk and Honey: A Year of Jewish Holidays* by Jane Yolen. The poem combines the imagery of the shofar with farming and herding.

It would be ideal if the third grade attempted to make a shofar. To make a shofar, the class teacher or representative would need to contact a sheep farm and ask about obtaining a horn from a slaughtered ram. In Michael Strassfeld's book *The Jewish Holidays: A Guide and Commentary*, Rabbi Zalman Schacter offers a "recipe" for making a shofar.

> Obtain a ram's horn. Boil it for three to five hours until you can remove the cartilage. Heat sand to 300–500 degrees and let the horn sit and sit and sit in the sand.

> Using insulated gloves, pick up the horn and bend it little by little until the fibers stretch. You have to straighten it out enough so that you can drill a hole to form the mouthpiece. When you have the shape you want, plunge the horn into cold water. Drill a hole for the mouthpiece until you reach the hollow part of the shofar.[34]

The school music director could be invited to help the class with this project.

If the class cannot make a shofar, then the teacher can contact a local synagogue to borrow one or, better yet, the school could buy one through one of the catalogs listed in the reference section. One colleague blew the shofar every day leading up to Rosh Hashanah, but she always did it at different times, so as to "wake up" the children. On Rosh Hashanah, when it is tradition to blow the shofar one hundred times, each of her twenty students had an opportunity to blow five blasts. They did this in the classroom, the playground, and the halls, and they delighted in waking up different areas of the school.

The shofar is a very difficult instrument to master. When trying to blow the shofar, the child may come up against his own impatience and the desire to give up. Inherent in symbolism of the shofar are the deeper meanings of both Yom Kippur and Michaelmas. If each grade had its own shofar to blow every autumn, then by eighth grade the children will have had time to conquer a very real "dragon."

By third grade the children will be able to understand some of the deeper elements of the high holiday rituals. Along with the regular blessings, the third grade may begin the ritual of Tashlikh. The children can gather up their crumbs from snack or lunch, and then at the end of the day the class can go to a nearby body of water (or even a bucket of water in the classroom) and cast away their crumbs. The teacher should talk about the ceremony of Tashlikh as a time to look back on how they acted last year in second grade and what things they wish to change about themselves for third grade. This may be a big leap for the third grade consciousness. The teacher might encourage a focus on more external things, such as being nicer to other children, trying to write neater, or not complaining about eurythmy. The children can become more introspective in later years.

For Yom Kippur the teacher can bring the picture of the ritual fast. Why, during the harvest time when there is plenty of food, would the people choose not to eat? On Yom Kippur the third grade could eat lunch or snack in silence and notice what happens. Ask them to listen to their own voices in their heads rather than the normal cacophony of voices around them. This type of silence is what the Jewish people strive for during Yom Kippur so that they can remember times they might have hurt someone else. By not eating they are not distracted and can focus on listening and praying and asking forgiveness from those they have hurt.

The Chasidic tale about the pillow is an appropriate picture for third grade. Now that they have more awareness of their surroundings, the third graders are less likely to hurt someone with a stick or a fist, but they are still not fully aware of how much their words can hurt others. When we tell the story of Genesis there is already a focus on the power of words. Later in the curriculum we begin looking at words more objectively through studying the parts of speech. The story of the pillow links the focus on words in third grade to the themes of Yom Kippur.

The teacher need not go much deeper into Yom Kippur at this time. This should be a time for the third graders to begin thinking about forgiveness in a simple way. In the activities I have done with third graders on this theme, I have found they are not quite ready to enter into the will of forgiveness. After presenting Yom Kippur, let the third graders sleep on forgiveness for another year.

Verses for Third Grade

ROSH HASHANAH IS HERE
    Rosh Hashanah is here at last—
    Sound the shofar. Give a blast!
    Le Shanah Tovah is the way
    To say, "Happy New Year" on this day.
              – Sylvia Rouss[35]

YOTZER OR
    The sun rose today.
    It will set this evening.
    Tomorrow the sun will rise again.
    The world goes on, day then night,
    Day then night.
    Winter changes into spring.
    Spring becomes summer.
    Summer turns into fall.
    Then winter happens again.
    A year happens every single year.
    Every day I get up and start again.
    Life comes in circles.
    I can learn from yesterday and change in time
    For tomorrow.
    The world goes on, day then night,
    Day then night.
              – Traditional[36]

A Sweet New Year[37]

by

Levin Kipnis

Far, far away where sky and earth appear to embrace each other the two sisters met. The older sister, Lady Lastyear, was old and weary. Her face was wrinkled, her clothing shabby. She moaned and groaned as she came trudging down the mountain to the valley below.

Her sister, Miss Newyear, was young and pretty. Dressed in a charming sky-blue dress with a beautiful wreath of flowers on her head, she stepped gracefully on her way to the top of the high mountain. Four angels accompanied Miss Newyear: one on her right, one on her left, one behind her, and one in front.[38]

"*Shalom*, my dear sister!" Miss Newyear greeted the old lady. "Why are you moaning and groaning?"

Lady Lastyear leaned heavily on her cane and replied with a deep sigh, "I am broken-hearted, dear sister! Things look very dark and hopeless!"

"And what can you tell me about our people in this wide world?" the younger sister asked.

"Oh, sad and bitter is their lot! Sad and bitter!" moaned the old lady.

Meanwhile the sun began to set, and Lady Lastyear resumed her trudging down the mountain while the youthful Miss Newyear skipped briskly on her way to the top.

Miss Newyear walked ahead, but she was still worried and saddened. "What else can I do to bring joy and sweetness to our people?" she kept asking herself.

A pomegranate grove appeared on the side of the mountain. Rows of trees stretched on the sides of the grove and among their sparkling and glittering leaves hung red-cheeked pomegranates.

"A happy and sweet new year!" wished the grove. "What causes you to look so sad and down-hearted, my dear?"

"My dear pomegranate grove!" replied Miss Newyear. "My heart aches and pains over the sad and bitter lot of our people all over the world."

"My pomegranates are ripe," said the grove, "and their juice is sweet. Take them and sweeten the lot of our people!"

At the command of Miss Newyear the third angel plucked the choicest pomegranates and carried them in a basket on his head.

Miss Newyear continued on her way, but could not put out of her mind her sister's words.

"Will these grapes and pomegranates be enough to gladden and sweeten the lot of our people who are scattered all over the wide world?" she asked herself.

Her thoughts were interrupted by the appearance of a huge beehive. A swarm of golden bees with transparent wings, big round eyes, and slender curved feelers surrounded the bewildered Miss Newyear.

"Zzzz....," buzzed the bees. "We flew from flower to flower gathering sweet honey. We stood in line from morning until sunset and worked without a stop—chewing, macerating and making the honeycombs. Our golden honey is sweet and its fragrance is heavenly. Take it, bring it to your people, and make their new year as sweet as our honey!"

The fourth angel accepted the honeycombs and carried them in a large jug.

The first three stars appeared in the sky when Miss Newyear and her accompanying angels reached the top of the mountain. The big city was decorated in their honor. All the houses were whitewashed. Doors and windows were repainted and covered with colorful curtains. White and blue flags waved from the balconies, and burning candles in each house spread cheer and merriment. Men and women were dressed in holiday clothes, and children wore their new suits and dresses. They filled the streets with laughter and songs.

Miss Newyear spread her wings over the city and sent her angels to deliver the sweets to every home. When the people returned to their homes from the synagogue, they sat around their tables, tasted the sweet grapes, ate the juicy pomegranate, dipped pieces of bread in honey, and wished each other, "A happy and sweet new year!"

THE ANNOUNCING TOOL[39]

by

Rabbi Marc Gellman

A long time ago when all people lived in one place, getting the news was easy. They had criers who would walk around town, and after no more than a morning of yelling everyone knew that something special had happened. But when people began living all over the place, even the criers could not spread the news far enough. Mostly, people just didn't get the news, but some special events had to be announced, and the arrival of a new year was the most special of all. So a man name Enoch asked God what to do to get the news of the new year around the world.

God said to Enoch, "You need a special announcing tool—go find one!" The next day Enoch returned with two rocks. "Listen to my fine announcing tool," he said and banged the two rocks together, making a loud rock-banging noise.

God said to Enoch, "What kind of announcing tool is this to tell of the arrival of the new year? Rocks do not make music, they only make noise. The new year is a time for music and singing, not banging and yelling." God frowned at Enoch, who scurried off to find a new announcing tool.

The next day Enoch returned with a gong. "Listen to my fine announcing tool which makes a beautiful sound," he said, and hit the gong, which made a gong-ringing sound.

God said to Enoch, "What kind of announcing tool is this to tell of the arrival of the new year? The gong does make a beautiful sound, but it is made of iron, and iron is used to make weapons of war. The new year is a time of peace, not war." God frowned at Enoch, who scurried off to find a new announcing tool.

The next day Enoch returned with a harp. "Listen to my fine announcing tool which makes a beautiful sound and is not made of iron!" Then Enoch strummed a tune on the harp.

God said to Enoch, "The harp also will not do as an announcing tool for the new year. The harp does indeed make beautiful sounds and it is not a weapon of war, but the harp is too soft a sound to announce the new year. The new year is a time of loud rejoicing and a loud announcing tool is needed, a tool that will carry the news of the new year from hilltop to hilltop around the world." God frowned at Enoch, who scurried off to find a new announcing tool.

The next day Enoch arrived with a golden trumpet. "Listen to my fine announcing tool which makes a beautiful sound, is not made of iron and is loud enough to carry the news from hilltop to hilltop." Then Enoch blew a loud note on the golden horn.

God said to Enoch, "The golden horn is a good announcing tool, but not good enough for the new year. True, the golden horn makes beautiful sounds, is not made of iron, and is loud enough; but the horn is not a natural instrument. It is made by people and not by Me. It is hollow, but not naturally hollow. It is made hollow by human hands. It makes a beautiful sound only after it has been pounded and shaped by human needs. The new year is not a time to glorify human creations. The new year is for all creatures, the animals and people as well. Find something to celebrate the new year which is for all My creatures." God frowned at Enoch, who scurried off to find a new announcing tool.

The next day Enoch was a little late in coming, but he finally arrived, a little out of breath. "I am embarrassed to present my new announcing tool. It is only a ram's horn—not nearly as beautiful as the golden horn, or as sweet and delicate as the harp—but it does make fine sounds, and is not a weapon of war, and is loud enough to get the news from hilltop to hilltop. I have done nothing to the horn; it is naturally hollow, and it comes from one of your creatures. But there is just one thing. All the other instruments were easy to make a sound with, but this ram's horn is impossible to play. I blow and blow, and then a toot comes out, and then nothing, and then maybe another toot comes out, and then nothing, and then maybe another toot. I wish it were easier." God smiled the biggest smile at Enoch, and then taught him how to blow the ram's horn for the big celebration of the new year which was soon to begin.

Chasidic Tale[40]

by

Joel Lurie Grishaver

The rabbi was very angry. Everywhere he went it was the same thing. All he heard was laughing. All over town, people were whispering and laughing—and the rabbi was getting angrier and angrier. He knew that Nathan was at home crying.

Nathan had done a foolish thing. Barukh had watched and laughed, and then told Golda and Fruma about the foolish thing that Nathan had done. They too, laughed. Fruma told Teyva, Yosi and Dan, who also laughed at Nathan's foolishness. Yosi had told Sarah who told Benjamin who told Penniah. All of them were laughing. Meanwhile, Golda had told her mother who told her best friend who told her husband who told everyone in his store the story of Nathan's foolish act. Everyone in the store laughed. All over town people were laughing and passing along the story of the foolish thing Nathan had done. Meanwhile Nathan was at home crying. That night, the rabbi heard a knock at this door. It was Barukh.

"I don't know what to do. Nathan won't talk to me. He used to be my best friend. Now, he slams the door in my face. All he says is, 'You hurt me.' I said I was sorry, but he wouldn't listen, all he would say was, 'You hurt me.'"

The rabbi understood. He had a plan. He told Barukh, "Meet me tomorrow at noon at the very top of the town clock tower. There I will teach you a great secret. But you must do one thing. You must bring a pillow with you. Without a pillow, I can't teach you anything."

Barukh was confused. He didn't understand. But he knew that he had to follow the rabbi's instructions. At noon they met at the top of the clock tower. They looked down over the whole village. The rabbi told Barukh to rip open the pillow. As soon as he began to tear, the wind began to grab the feathers and carry them away. The rabbi took the pillow out of Barukh's hands. He shook it. The air was filled with feathers. The wind carried them all over town. They blew into the market place and past the school windows. They blew into the backyards and onto the porch outside Golda's mother's best friend's husband's store. Everywhere. The whole town was filled with feathers. The rabbi then said, "Go and gather up all the feathers."

But—that's impossible! No one could do that.

Then the rabbi said, "Then go and gather up the story about the foolish thing which Nathan did."

But—that's impossible! No one could do that.

He was silent. He thought. Then finally he said, "I understand."

Rosh Hashanah and Yom Kippur in the Fourth Grade

After a full year of working with the stories of the Torah in the third grade, the children now carry a picture of the Hebrew people into their experience of the Jewish holidays. As Rosh Hashanah and Yom Kippur approach, the teacher may choose to do some recall with her class and retell the story of Isaac. If the teacher was unable to get to the story of Jonah during third grade, this would be an appropriate time to bring it to the class. However, it is more conducive to the yearly rhythm of the children to let these stories sleep for a year. Instead the children can experience Rosh Hashanah through new stories and activities that support the fourth grade curriculum.

The Norse myths tell of a time with many gods rather than one God and set the stage for fractions in the mathematics block. Another way to lay some groundwork for fractions is for the fourth grade to experiment with the sounds of the shofar. The shofar has four calls; *Tekiah, Shevarim, Teru'ah* and *Tekiah Gedolah. Tekiah* is one long blow. *Shevarim* is three short blows. *Teru'ah* is nine quick blows. *Tekiah Gedolah* is one very long blow. Shown pictorially, they look like this: [41]

Tekiah _____
Shevarim ____   ____   ____
Teru'ah _ _ _   _ _ _   _ _ _
Tekiah Gedolah _____

As you can see, this is representative of fractions. We have one whole, thirds and ninths. *Tekiah Gedolah* is as long as all the others put together, so it also shows thirds.

The fourth grade can use lummy sticks, hand clapping, or their own voices to try to represent the different sounds of the shofar. The whole class can try each sound on its own first. Next the class can be split into groups so that one group begins as *Tekiah*, then *Shevarim* and *Teru'ah* follow. It will definitely be a will exercise for the children to hold onto their rhythm and fit it into the other rhythms. This is also a good group cooperation activity. It is not necessary at this time to relate the blows to fractions. Right now the children should just have the experience of doing (will) and later the teacher can refer to the activity. Once they have started the fraction block, the teacher can ask the children if anyone can give an example of an activity they already did this year that relates to fractions. The children may remember the shofar activity, or there may be an element of surprise in recalling it!

The Rosh Hashanah story for fourth grade is a creation story adapted from Midrash. "The Never-Ending Song" is an imagination of creation prior to the advent of man. It is a perfect bridge between the creation imagery of the Torah and the creation imagery of the Norse. The pictures of the animal kingdom can be recalled later when teaching the Human and Animal block. There are creatures of land, sea and air who set the tone for the coming of man. This story is reminiscent of Steiner's work with the images of Lion, Eagle, and Bull, and it also includes the simpler creatures like the starfish. Finally, this story ends with a message that meets the development of the fourth grader and is also much needed in our time.

After a year in the Hebrew bible, the children should be more familiar with the themes of Yom Kippur. At this stage, the ten-year-old is able to start taking responsibility for his actions. This is part of Loki's teachings in the Norse myths. The class should be able to do the following beeswax activity that touches upon the crucial elements of Yom Kippur.

Turn the lights off in the room. If you did not tell the third grade Chasidic tale last year, tell it now. If you did tell it, remind the children that Yom Kippur is the time when the Jewish people remember when they have done something that hurt someone else. In fourth grade the teacher can also talk about how we sometimes do things that hurt ourselves (which speaks directly to some children with discipline issues). Each child is then given a strip of paper approximately eight inches long and one-half inch wide. The children should also be given each a piece of beeswax that they can warm in their armpits while writing. On one side of the paper they write, "I forgive_____ for_____." It should be made clear to the children that they do not have to share what they write with anyone else, this is just for their eyes. Once they have completed the writing, they should roll the paper up into a tight cylinder. The children should then make a vessel out of the beeswax with an opening large enough to fit the rolled paper. The paper is inserted into the beeswax and the container can then be sealed or left open with just a little of the paper showing. Some may wish to embellish the vessel or turn it into a budding flower.

The teacher then tells the students that they should each take his/her vessel home and put in a place where it will be seen every day. It will serve as a reminder that they actually forgave someone and can no longer hold onto the anger they felt towards that person. It is an important aspect of Yom Kippur that we not just say we forgive, but that we actually let go of the old feelings and begin afresh with those who hurt us and those whom we have hurt. The ten-year-old is ready to act in an "upright" way, and this activity encourages that behavior. This activity, along with the Rosh Hashanah verse, kindles the types of reflections on our humanity that will be uncovered later in the Human and Animal block as part of the uniqueness of humans.

Rosh Hashanah Verse for Fourth Grade

Rosh Hashanah Eve
    Stale moon, climb down.
    Clear the sky.
    Get out of town.
    Good-bye.
    Fresh moon, arise.
    Throw a glow.
    Shine a surprise.
    Hello
    New Year, amen.
    Now we begin:
    Teach me to be a new me.
           – Harry Phillip[42]

The Never-Ending Song[43]

by

Nina Jaffe

Long, long ago, before the day human beings were created, all the creatures of the world were beginning to populate the earth and the sky. The greatest of all the birds was the Ziz. Her wings were as wide as the sky itself. When she stretched them out to fly, she could reach from one end of the earth to the other. It was the Ziz who, with her shining golden feathers, protected the earth from the hot winds of the south. Once, the egg of a Ziz broke and it flooded the forest and even the mountaintops!

Of the beasts of the field, the largest of all was Behemoth. His bones were as strong as brass. His legs were like great iron bars. He could drink the Jordan River with a single gulp and every day he grazed in the pastures of a magic mountain. When he finished eating in the evening, there was not a single blade of grass left to be seen, and yet, in the morning the meadows were lush and green again. His tail was as strong as a great cedar tree, and when he walked about, the earth trembled beneath him. Behemoth kept his home in a cave in the magic mountain, near the nesting place of his friend, the Ziz.

In the swirling waters of the sea lived the greatest sea monster of all time—Leviathan. He has as many eyes as the year has days, and scales that shone brighter than the sun itself. When Leviathan roamed the deep, one swish of his tail would cause huge tidal waves. Smoke poured from his nostrils and the water boiled and bubbled in his wake.

These were the great creatures of the sky and earth and sea, and they kept to themselves. At night, Leviathan would curl his tail around the ocean and sleep by the shores of the magic mountain, near his friends, Ziz and Behemoth, while up in the heavens, the angels sang them sweet lullabies.

But the Holy One had also put many other kinds of flying and creeping things in the world, large and small, and they were all trying to get used to their new homes. The small creatures were not having an easy time of it. The robins and sparrows were constantly being chased down by the great birds of prey—the eagles, hawks, owls, and condors. Day after day, they found their nests had been robbed, and many of them were carried away in sharp talons, never to return.

The great sharks and barracudas never stopped feasting on the little fish. Wherever they turned, minnows and goldfish, guppies and trout were being hunted down in every corner of the ocean, in every lake, and in every river. On land, the lions and tigers, the great wolves and panthers were always at the heels of the mice and rabbits. The deer, the zebra, and the gentle giraffes never had a moment to rest from their running. In all the earth, there was no place to hide. The very world itself was being disturbed by the antics of small spirits and demons who ran about, hither and thither, turning mountains upside down and twisting the rivers out of shape.

Finally, all of the small creatures met together to talk over their problems. Something had to be done! Chittering and squawking, meowing and squeaking, they came to a spot that they all agreed might be safe, at least for a little while—by the roots of a great tree that stood near a gently flowing stream.

The rabbit spoke first. "We can't go on like this!" he cried. "There is no rest for me or my family. We are always running from some big animal!"

"You are right," croaked the frog. "Surely the Holy One did not create us to live like this!"

"We know that some of us must be eaten," chirped the sparrow. "After all, I myself must live on the bugs and insects. But if the hunting never stops, we will all disappear, and there will be no creatures left but the great beasts of prey!"

"You are right again," croaked the frog. "But what can we do?"

The animals, birds, and fish twittered and cheeped together for some time, but no one could come up with an idea. Finally, from the bottom of the stream, a little starfish made her way to the top. "Shhh," she whispered, "listen to me."

"Shhh," cried all the creatures. "Let us listen to the starfish."

And the starfish began, "My friends, I have been pushed by the currents of the water to many places on the earth. One day, a great wave washed me up on the shores of a shining beach. Near it stood a great mountain. I saw three enormous creatures. None of you has ever seen creatures so great or so powerful, and as the sun went down, the angels sang them to sleep. Perhaps they could help us."

The animals and the birds agreed that each would send a representative to follow the starfish to the shores by the magic mountain. For what else could they do?

The mouse and sparrow followed the starfish as she made her way to the magic mountain. Just at sundown, Ziz and Leviathan were about to take their rest (Behemoth had already gone into his cave), when they heard three tiny voices calling to them from the sandy shore. "Please wake up, oh great creatures! It is only us, mouse, sparrow, and starfish, and we wish to speak with you."

Slowly, Leviathan uncurled his tail. Ziz fluttered and fluffed her wings, and Behemoth peeped out of his cave. "What do you wish, little ones?' they asked in one voice.

"Oh, great ones, if you please," cried the mouse, "we have come to ask for help."

"Yes," said the starfish. "All over the world, the beasts and birds of prey and the hungry sharks stalk us little animals without ceasing. Spiteful demons are turning the mountains upside down. They are twisting the streams and rivers in all directions, just to confuse us. We are afraid that our kind will never have a chance to live in this beautiful world that the Holy One has created."

"That is why we have come," cheeped the sparrow. "Isn't there anything you can do?"

Leviathan blinked his hundreds of eyes. Behemoth sniffed into the winds, and Ziz curled her mighty talons. For some time, they were silent. Then, they took counsel with the angels who were looking down from the starry heavens, and there was no sound of sweet lullabies that night. "It is time for the Great Words," they whispered among themselves.

"Yes," the angels agreed, "it is time."

Finally they turned to the little ones and spoke again, in one voice, "Yes, little friends. There is something we can do. Return to your homes now and wait."

The mouse, the sparrow, and the starfish hurried back to give the message to all their friends.

That year, in the month of Tammuz, when the air was hot and the summer sun burned down, Behemoth stepped out of his cave. He lifted his great head and roared so loudly that the lions stopped in their tracks. His tail hit the ground with such force that the earth shook, and the tigers and wolves, the panthers and the jaguars trembled in their skins. They hid their heads in their paws and listened to the sound of the Word as it entered their very hearts.

The sound of the roar echoed on through the months of Av and Elul, until the autumn month of Tishri. Then the Ziz unfurled her enormous wings and uttered a cry that pierced through the very clouds of the sky. At the sound of that great cry, the eagles and hawks, the condors and the owls stopped in their flights, stunned and afraid. For the very first time, they felt pity and stopped their hunting for a time. They joined with the Ziz and called out her Word in hoots and screeches until the winter month of Tevet.

Then, Leviathan raised his shining tusks from the depths of the sea. He whipped up the waves into a foaming froth that shook the barracudas and the swordfish from their path of destruction and hummed his Word into the ears of the sharks and killer whales. Out from behind the rocks and underwater crannies swam the little fish, lighting up the waters with flashes of silver, red, and gold. They listened as the big fish passed on the word through the currents of the oceans and streams as Shevat went by, and the Adar, until the gentle spring breezes of the month of Nisan blew in.

In the heavens, the angels gathered their voices together and sang their Word through the spheres until the demons bowed their heads in awe. The spirits put down the hills and mountains and let the rivers follow their own courses.

Ever since that time, the creatures of the earth have lived together, taking what they needed and no more, giving each other times of rest and play as well as times of hunting and fear. For the word of Behemoth was "Peace," and the word of the Ziz was "Justice." The word of Leviathan was "Mercy," and the word of the angels was "Love."

This is an ancient chant that circles the earth that all animals, birds, and fish listen to and obey. Of course, all this happened before the time that human beings were created. But if you ever find yourself in a quiet place, in the woods or by the sea, and you listen very carefully, you too may hear the echoes of this never-ending song.

[Note from Ms. Jaffe: "The Never-Ending Song" is adapted from the Midrash. Midrashim are stories, parables, and legends told by the rabbis of old in order to explain or elaborate on passages from the Torah. In this story, we read of mythical beasts and monsters named Ziz, Behemoth, and Leviathan. The origin of these names goes back to ancient times. The Jews of the Near East were influenced by the mythology and cultures of the people who surrounded them—the Egyptians, Babylonians, and Canaanites. These mythic images found their way into the stories and writings of the ancient Hebrew and became incorporated into lore and legend, taking on their own unique significance in Jewish culture. Mention of these creatures can be found in the books of Genesis, Psalms, Job, and other texts dating back to the first century.]

Source: *Legends of the Bible* by Louis A. Ginzberg

Rosh Hashanah and Yom Kippur in the Fifth Grade

The fifth grade is a time ripe for deep reflection on the true meaning of "awe." The fifth grade students embark on a journey through the ancient civilizations of Persia, India, Egypt and Greece. As they learn about these amazing times and peoples, a sense of awe will awaken in the children. As the school year begins and Rosh Hashanah arrives, the teacher can set a tone for the whole year by focusing on "awe." The teacher can help the class understand what they are really saying when they call something "awesome." As the class moves beyond the limits of their colloquial relationship to this word, they should then be able to experience (through feelings) a true sense of awe as they move through this year's curriculum. Having been exposed to Rosh Hashanah and Yom Kippur for five years, the class should begin to understand why these holidays are called the "Days of Awe."

Fifth graders are also moving into pre-adolescence and their behavior will reflect this developmental transition. The stories for Rosh Hashanah and Yom Kippur relate well to this bridge of development between childhood and pre-adolescence.

The fifth grade curriculum moves the children towards a more alert consciousness. While the Ancient cultures were awestruck by their rulers (pharaohs, gods), the Greeks began to wrestle more with their surroundings, moving beyond complacency to awaken the individual mind. The Chasidic tale about the fire is a parable about this need to awaken and begin problem-solving in the world around us. The teacher can tell the story and ask the children what they experience as "alarms." How do they know when they are getting off track? How do they catch themselves? These questions relate to their inner life, but also practical life. How do they catch a math or spelling error? What checks have they put in place? If this awareness is missing in some students, this would be a good year to build a foundation so that when the more demanding work of the upper school "ignites," they will know how to alter their work habits.

If the fourth grade story, "The Never-Ending Song," was not told last year, the teacher may tell it this year for Rosh Hashanah. As related in the author's note at the end of the story, this tale has its origins with the Jews of the Near East who were influenced by the Egyptians, Babylonians, and Canaanites, and thus integrates well into the themes of this year's curriculum.

The Yom Kippur parable speaks to the task of each individual in a group to become conscious of his thoughts and actions. This is an appropriate picture for fifth grade. The overview of the caste system in India and then the different philosophical schools in Greece reflect a type of group unity that may not always be most beneficial for the individual. The fifth grader may also begin to struggle more with peer pressure. The desire to fit in or the fear of standing out may even affect school performance. Various studies of pre-adolescent and adolescent girls found that at this age many girls who were academically superior to boys began purposely under-achieving in order to stay part of the group.[44] A fine story that is also recommended for this age is "The Herdsman's Whistle" by Jane Yolen from her book *Milk and Honey*. This story poignantly shows that those who stay true to themselves are the ones who are most rewarded.

Verse for Fifth Grade

> Sound of the Trumpet
> The shofar, symbol of the new year, blows;
> The tone resounds, and hopeful mankind knows
> It is the call of peace that's yet to be
> A long-drawn note of all humanity.
> – Fania Kruger[45]

Sounding an Alarm: A Rosh Hashanah Parable[46]

by

Judyth Saypol

Once it happened that a man from a small village came to the big city for the first time. In the middle of the night he was awakened by the loud beating of drums. He asked the innkeeper what the noise meant. He was told that when a fire breaks out, the people beat their drums, and before long the fire is gone.

When the man returned home, he told the village leaders about this wonderful system for putting out fires. The people were excited and ordered drums for every household.

The next time a fire broke out, the people beat their drums. As they waited for the fire to go out, many homes burned to the ground. A visitor asked what was happening. When told of the fire and the drums, he exclaimed, "Do you think a fire can be put out by beating drums? They only sound an alarm so people will wake up and go to the well for water to put out the fire."

[Blowing the shofar is also an alarm encouraging us to change our ways.]

Rosh Hashanah and Yom Kippur in the Sixth Grade

In sixth grade there is a move toward law and order after the "hedonism" of fifth grade. The children study Rome, for instance, with an emphasis on justice. Now civilians must be accountable not only to their gods, but also to each other. To support this piece of the curriculum, the Days of Awe can lead to a study of the true significance of accountability. The teacher can ask the students how they think God judges us and how we judge both ourselves and others. What is a fair way to judge someone else? What is a kind way to judge ourselves? This type of reflecting also relates to the study of Christ's entrance into the world and the compassionate being he represents. How do we cultivate compassion and forgiveness?

The teacher can revisit the beeswax activity from fourth grade. This time in addition to writing on the paper, "I forgive _____ for _____," the student should write on the other side, "I forgive myself for _____." At this age the students are aware of ways in which they may sabotage themselves by their own behavior. Some students may already have been disciplined through suspension or loss of privileges and may not have thought their treatment fair. Have the students look back on ways they have hurt themselves over the past year. The act of forgiveness for their actions should incite a consciousness, which will invoke, we hope, ownership and change.

Another suitable activity for sixth grade that again relates to the Christian ideal is *Tikkun O'Lam*. Tikkun O'Lam means "repair of the world" and is part of the consciousness of the Days of Awe. At Rosh Hashanah, Jews are expected to do *Tzedakah*, charity. The sixth grade class can go to a senior center, a homeless shelter, or a low-income day care center and provide apples and honey, sing, and play their instruments. If this is not possible, the class could sponsor a food or clothing drive.

For Yom Kippur, the teacher can show how the Day of Atonement is really the Day of At-One-Ment. What is the difference between atoning and being at-one-with? This also relates to the monastic life that they will study this year. Some children may be surprised when they see this word broken down. Encourage the class to find other words that may have other meanings within them. (This is also a natural introduction to word etymology.)

We see the sixth grade year as reflecting the differences between the two aspects of the Days of Awe. Rosh Hashanah is like Rome, boisterous in its presentation, while Yom Kippur thrives in the solemnity that is a part of the Middle Ages.

Verse for Sixth Grade

> THE NEW YEAR
> No bells ring through the midnight air,
>   No sound of vulgar revelry,
> But everywhere the trumpet blares,
>   Sends greetings over land and sea.
>
> And in the Jewish household reigns
>   A quiet born of pious thought;
> And every Jewish heart attains
>   A joy from festive feelings wrought.
>
> No ribald shout, no coarse play
>   Proclaims Rosh Hashanah is here.
> But we hope and smile and pray,
>   In this wise greet the glad New Year!
>   – Abraham Burstein[47]

The Legend of the Jewish Pope[48]

by

Micha Bin Gorion

Once upon a time in the city of Mainz which is situated on the River Rhine, there lived a famous teacher, and his name was Rabbi Shimeon. In his house there were three mirrors, and everybody could see in them what had happened in the world before and what would happen in the future. When Rabbi Shimeon died, a well sprang up from his grave. This was considered a great miracle, since the water had healing powers.

Rabbi Shimeon had a son and his name was Elchanan. When he was yet little, his father and his mother went to the house of worship and the boy was left under the supervision of a young maid. As usual, a woman from the neighborhood came to prepare the stove for the family, and when she came, she took the child from the cradle, put him into her arms, and left. The maid thought nothing ill of it, for she believed that the woman had gone out to play with the child and would soon return. Yet return she did not, but took the child to a place far away and gave him to the priest of the church.

When Rabbi Shimeon and his wife returned, they found neither child nor maid, for she had run out of the house to look for the boy. When she did not find him, she returned weeping and reported what had happened. Then the parents raised their voices and wept and cried out in overwhelming pain. Rabbi Shimeon fasted and chastised his body day and night. He prayed to God that He should return his son to him, but the prayers went unheeded. And the Lord refused to reveal the name of the place where the boy was.

In the meantime Elchanan grew up among the priests, and his wisdom and his scholarship grew with him, for he took after his father and had an open and quick mind for learning. He went from one university to the other until his wisdom was exceedingly great, and at long last he came to Rome. Here he learned many more languages than he already knew and acquired a great reputation as a scholar. Soon thereafter he was elevated to the position of cardinal. His fame soon extended all over the world and everybody wanted to see him because he was so handsome and so learned. It was at this time that the Pontiff of the Roman Church died and nobody was considered worthier to become his successor than the cardinal. Thus the son of Rabbi Shimeon of Mainz became the Pope of Rome.

There is no doubt that the new Pope knew about his Jewish origin, and he even knew that his father was the great Rabbi Shimeon who lived in the city of Mainz which was situated on the River Rhine. But his reputation and the high position which he held forced him to disregard his yearning, which grew more and more insistent, and he was anxious to see his father face to face. Thus he decided to use a ruse to bring his father to Rome. He sent a papal decree to the Bishop of Mainz and asked him to inform the Jews of the city that from now on they would not be permitted to celebrate the Sabbath or to circumcise their newborn sons, and the women were no longer allowed to observe the law of purity which had been held in high esteem by the Jews. The new Pope thought in his heart: When this decree is read to the Jews of Mainz, they will soon send a delegation of worthy men to ask me to rescind the order, and there is no doubt that the group will be headed by my father.

That is what happened. The Jews of Mainz were frightened when the Bishop read the papal decree to them. They implored him to avert the evil, but he told them that he had no power to do so and advised them to go see the Pope. The Jews of Mainz did penitence and fasted and prayed to the Lord, and then they elected two scholars who would accompany Rabbi Shimeon on his mission to Rome.

When the three delegates came to Rome, they went to the Jewish quarter and told the brethren of the purpose which had brought them to Rome. At first the Jews of Rome did not believe it, for the Pope had been known to be a friend of the Jews. But then Rabbi Shimeon showed them the papal decree, and the Roman Jews said, "Woe unto us, for the Lord is wroth at you." And they called a day of fasting and prayed for the welfare of their brethren from Mainz.

After this, they went to a cardinal who saw the Pope daily and told him about the matter. The cardinal advised that the Jews from Mainz should put their complaint in writing. He would then submit it to the Pope.

When the letter was given to the Pope, he looked at the signatures and discovered that Rabbi Shimeon, his father, was among the delegates. He invited them to come to the papal palace. Soon Rabbi Shimeon stood face to face with the Pontiff of the Roman Church. He prostrated himself before him, but the Pope asked him to rise and to sit on a chair. Then he asked him to make his plea. Rabbi Shimeon could hardly speak because of the tears that choked his voice, but he spoke freely about the decree which threatened his community. The Pope did not respond immediately, but he began to engage Rabbi Shimeon in a learned dispute, and the rabbi marveled at the scholarship of the Pontiff. Knowing that the rabbi was a famous chess player, the Pope invited him to play, and to Shimeon's amazement he beat him handsomely after only a few moves. But by then the Pope could no longer hold back. He asked everybody present to leave and then told Rabbi Shimeon that he was his son. He explained that the decree had been but a ruse to make him come to Rome so that he could see him. He gave Rabbi Shimeon a papal letter which rescinded the decree, bade him farewell, and let him return to Mainz in peace.

After many years passed, the Pope disappeared from Rome and clandestinely returned to Mainz. Return he did, not merely to the place of his birth, but also to the God of his fathers. There is a hymn that is recited on the second day of the Jewish New Year, written by Rabbi Shimeon, describing the story of the Jewish Pope. Nobody should doubt its veracity, for it really happened.

Repentant Jews: A Parable[49]

As Rabbi Levi Isaac of Berditchev and his sexton were going to the synagogue for the *Selihot* services on the eve of Rosh Hashanah, a sudden downpour made them seek shelter under the awning of a tavern. The sexton peered through one of the windows and saw a group of Jews feasting, drinking, and reveling. He impatiently urged Levi Isaac to see for himself how the Jews were behaving when they should be in the synagogue praying to God for forgiveness of their sins.

Disregarding the sexton's urging, the rabbi chided him, "It is forbidden to derogate the children of Israel. They are surely reciting the benedictions for food and drink. May God bless these loyal Jews."

The disillusioned sexton continued to peep into the tavern and eavesdrop. "Woe to us, rabbi!" the sexton exclaimed. "I just heard two of the Jews telling each of thefts they committed."

"If that be so, they are truly observant Jews," Levi Isaac joyfully admonished his sexton. "They are confessing their sins before Rosh Hashanah. As you know, no one is more righteous than he who repents."

Rosh Hashanah and Yom Kippur in the Seventh Grade

There is a departure from the familiar in the seventh grade's celebration of the Jewish holidays. Beginning with Rosh Hashanah and Yom Kippur, the seventh graders come to know the Jews of the Sepharad. The Sephardic Jews lived in Spain until the Inquisition and then dispersed around the globe. They spoke Hebrew and *Ladino*, a dialect of Spanish unique to the Jewish population. Their customs and traditions have persevered even though they seemed destined to evaporate into the sea winds of the Age of Exploration.

In the Sephardic tradition, it is customary to have a *Seder* for Rosh Hashanah. The seventh grade can have a snack or lunch with these symbolic foods. First there is wine (juice) and challah, as in past years. These blessings are done in Hebrew only. Then there are apples, leeks, beets or spinach, dates, pumpkin or squash, and finally, a whole fish including the head. The apples are for a good and sweet year. The leeks make sure that our luck does not lack (nor leak) in the coming year. Beets keep those who have harmed (beaten) us in the past from harming us again. Dates are for dating the beginning of a new year as one of happiness and peace. Squash is for a year that is full (like the gourd) of blessings. The fish ensures that we may move forward and upward, not backward, into the coming year.[50] The teacher can have all these foods on a plate and ask the students to guess what they symbolize. This culinary experience can be recalled later when discussing metaphor as part of Wish, Wonder and Surprise.

The teacher can ask the Spanish teacher to give the Ladino verses for dictation. Later the class teacher can put the verses on the board and have the children compare the Spanish they are learning with the Ladino versions. What is the same? What sounds the same but is spelled quite differently? The teacher could ask the class why they think the Jews of Spain created a language of their own that was similar and yet distinct. When the class studies Geography, the teacher can talk about the challenges of the Jews who spoke Ladino amidst Africans and Asians. This can lead to an interesting conversation about how to keep one's own identity while still assimilating into a group, a very appropriate topic for this age.

Verse for Seventh Grade

> THE JEWISH YEAR
> Our year begins with burnished leaves
>   That flame in frost and rime,
> With purple grapes and golden sheaves
>   In harvest time.
>
> Our year begins with biting cold,
>   With winds and storms and rain;
> The new year of the Jew grows old
>   In strife and pain.
>
> When others say the year has died,
>   We say the year is new,
> And we arise with power and pride
>   To prove it true.
>
> And we begin where others end,
>   And fight where others yield.
> And all the year we work and tend
>   Our harvest field.
>
> And after days of stormy rain
>   And days of drought and heat,
> When those that toiled have reaped their grain,
>   And all's complete
>
> Oh, then, when God has kept His word,
>   In peace we end our year.
> Our fruit is certain from the Lord.
>   We shall not fear.
>   – Jessie E. Sampter [51]

Verses in Ladino for Seventh Grade

SELICHOT PRAYERS

Non mas estes durmiendo adormesido
Desha tu kamino enmalesido
Alongate de tu uzo aboresido
Y siguie los caminos de tu enaltesido
Corre por seguir al fuerte de la antiguedad
Sigun corren las estreas dela claridad.[52]

O sleeper, sleep no more. Forsake your errant ways.
Leave far man's earthen tread, aspire to lofty paths.
Run swift as shining stars to serve the Rock of old.[53]

Por estudiar loke ay en los sielos despertar
Sus ovras mira de examinar
Observa onde prefero el Dio de morar
Y sus tiendas onde izo fixar
Mira a sus salvasiones de esperar
Ante ke el tiempo te araste
Y tu corason de azer su dover falte.[54]

Behold His skies, his fingers' vast work.
Gaze towards His high abode upheld by tireless arms.
Behold the starry gems inset in heaven's rings, and stand
in reverent awe,
and hope for saving grace, lest fate upcast your soul
and your heart becomes proud.[55]

SEPHARDIC BLESSING OVER WINE/JUICE

Baruch ata Adonay Eloenu melech aolam bore peri age-
fen.

LADINO BLESSING OVER THE APPLES AND HONEY

Sea aveluntado delante de ti Adonai nuestro Dio y Dio
de nuestros padres, ke se renove
sovre nozotros anyada buena y dulse,
de presipio de el anyo y asta kavo de el anyo.

May it be Thy will, Lord our God and God
of our fathers, to renew
upon us a good and sweet year,
from the beginning of the year until the end of the year.[56]

Rosh Hashanah and Yom Kippur in the Eighth Grade

Ideally the eighth grader has by now had ample exposure to the Jewish holidays. Part of the work of the final year in the grades is to review all that has come before. As the eighth graders prepare to begin anew and perhaps leave the classmates with whom they have journeyed, it is good to review what it means, and feels like, to end one cycle and begin another. What have been the cycles within the eight-year cycle that the class has shared? It might also be an appropriate time to talk about the fear that sometimes accompanies the excitement one feels when starting something new. What are the ways we can move through that fear (Saint George holding at bay rather than slaying the dragon)?

For Yom Kippur, the eighth grader can reflect on a whole history of relationships with classmates. Are there people with whom they struggled and are now close friends? Are there issues that are still unresolved? Now may be the opportune time to address them. Yom Kippur can also be a time to reflect on how the class has changed. The teacher and the class can share anecdotes from earlier years as a way to see what has stayed the same and what has changed, both consciously and unconsciously. It would be nice for the teacher to also recount the changes that occurred through actual striving on the part of the students.

During this time of definite rebellion and adolescence, the class can read together the prayer *Ki Hinneh Ka-Homer*. They can discuss, or write about, the idea that we are malleable instruments for something greater than ourselves. Do they agree? The class can also review Tikkun O'Lam in light of this prayer. If the word "sin" in this poem is too heavy-handed for the class, the teacher could substitute the word "transgression."

Both of the Jewish holiday stories recall the seventh grade Exploration block. Many teachers choose not to delve much into the Inquisition during seventh grade. This is understandable because the students should experience the wonder of that time more than the evil of that time. Now in eighth grade, with the Revolution curriculum, the stories about the Inquisition can be brought, shedding new light onto something now familiar. The two stories are about individual rebellion and risk taking, which could lead to good discussion as well as individual written responses. Both stories show courage under grave situations, as well as a courage that comes forth because of the desire to help others. This is surely the covenant we are asked to fulfill.

Verse for Eighth Grade

> KI HINNEH KA-HOMER
> LIKE THE CLAY IN THE HAND OF THE POTTER
>
> Like the clay in the hand of the potter
> Who thickens or thins it at his will,
> So are we in Thy hand, gracious God.
> Forgive our sin, Thy covenant fulfill.
>
> Like a stone in the hand of the mason
> Who preserves or breaks it at his will,
> So are we in Thy hand, Lord of life.
> Forgive our sin, Thy covenant fulfill.
>
> Like iron in the hand of the craftsman
> Who forges or cools it at his will,
> We are in Thy hand, our Keeper.
> Forgive our sin, Thy covenant fulfill.
>
> Like the wheel in the hand of the seaman
> Who directs or holds it at his will,
> So are we in Thy hand, loving God.
> Forgive our sin, Thy covenant fulfill.

Like the glass in the hand of the blower
Who dissolves or shapes it at his will,
So are we in Thy hand, God of grace.
Forgive our sin, Thy covenant fulfill.

Like the cloth in the hand of the tailor
Who smoothes or drapes it at his will,
So are we in Thy hand, righteous God.
Forgive our sin, Thy covenant fulfill.

Like silver in the hand of the smelter
Who refines or blends it at his will,
So are we in Thy hand, our Healer.
Forgive our sin, Thy covenant fulfill.
— Traditional[57]

Dona Gracia Nasi Mendes: An Ethical Will[58]

by

Annette Labovitz

Her Hebrew name was Channa, and she was born in Lisbon, Portugal, fourteen years after the expulsion of the Jews from that country. Her family was wealthy and distinguished; her elder brother was a physician at the royal court and he taught medicine at the university. The family was *converso*, secret Jews who publicly professed Christianity. The Spanish and the Portuguese called them *marranos*, meaning pigs, or those who marred true faith. The Hebrew word for them is *anusim*, forced to accept another religion. Eventually the family fled and returned to Judaism, becoming ardent supporters of Jewish life in Moslem-ruled lands and in Eretz Yisrael. But when we first meet the family of "La Senora," as she was known, they are still hiding in Lisbon from the Inquisition.

From a letter that was passed down from generation to generation, it is possible to decipher the terror under which the Jews in general, and the Gracia family in particular, lived during the Inquisition, that awesome period of time when they were not permitted to live in the Iberian peninsula (Spain and Portugal). "My name is Yosef, son of Avigdor, grandson of Menachem. I am writing this letter as an ethical will with the instructions that you read it every year on Rosh Hashanah in order that you thank God for our family being miraculously delivered from suffering and torment at the hands of the Inquisition.

"I worked as a servant in one of the cloisters. On the eve of Rosh Hashanah, the bishop called me and said, 'Listen to me, my child, you are undoubtedly true to the Church. I want you to perform a secret mission in order to prove just how faithful you really are. It is imperative that we true Christians weed out the heretics from the faithful, you know, the Jews that pretend to be Christians but profess their Judaism in the privacy of their homes. I want you to spy on the family of Don Gabriel Gracia and watch their every move. After you have been in his house a while, you will return to me and tell me everything that you saw there. You must be very careful not to divulge the reason for your being in his house, for, after all, he is a very important and distinguished person in this country. If he should suspect that you are spying, he will report you to the king. The king will be furious that one of his courtiers is suspect, and he will turn the slanderer over to the Inquisition. If you are tortured, you might implicate me in your confession, so I warn you to be very careful! The reason that I am asking you to do this is because I suspect Don Gabriel is a heretic and I need evidence.'

"I could not refuse to do the bidding of the bishop. I also knew that suspected heretics were tortured until they confessed, and then burned at the stake. I prayed that I would find nothing in the house of Don Gabriel to tell the bishop.

"That evening, I headed for his mansion. It was located in that section of Lisbon where the very wealthy lived. With great trepidation, I approached the gate. The gatekeeper recognized me and admitted me to the study. 'Please wait here,' he said. 'I will go upstairs and inform my master that you are here.'

"About an hour later, Don Gabriel descended the long winding staircase, and graciously extended his hand to welcome me. I examined his face carefully. On the surface, he was poised and cheerful, but he bore the wrinkles of a person who had been challenged over and over throughout his lifetime. I wondered why. He put his arm around me, guided me up the staircase, and we entered a dining room whose table was set elegantly with gold and silver vessels, as if for a very important banquet. He responded to my quizzical expression by saying, 'This party is being celebrated in honor of my father. Of course, you will join us.' I compared the ascetic life I led in the monastery with the luxury in this house. Throughout the meal, my thoughts were in turmoil. I had been sent to spy on this family, to find out if they were heretics, but I didn't want to turn anyone over to the Inquisition.

"When the meal ended, and everyone was satisfied with the best food and drink, I excused myself. I wanted to find a place to hide on the premises, hoping that I would have nothing to report. I hid near a corner of the big mansion on the outside, in order to have a clear view of their comings and goings. It did not take very long for me to notice a servant prepare the carriage, and Don Gabriel, his father and his son climbed into it. Their progress was very slow. I ran behind the carriage for a while through the very crowded streets. Not wanting to lose sight of them, I finally found an empty carriage that I hired to follow them. They never noticed me behind them. They drove to the outskirts of the city, instructed the servant to wait for them, and alighted. Slowly, they followed a path, deeper and deeper and deeper into the woods. I was right behind them. When they stopped, I sought refuge behind a broad-branched tree with a thick trunk. I was curious. Why had these people feasted and then come to the forest?

"I waited patiently, my pulse beating faster and faster. What were they doing? What would I tell the bishop? Would I be able to relate their suspicious actions in order that suspicion not fall upon me?

"Within the hour, the group of people had grown. I thought that, even from the distance, I recognized one of them to be Don Pedro, the treasurer to General Benedict. The people sat on small piles of twigs and tree branches. They removed small books from their pockets and began to mumble and shake fervently. After a while Don Gabriel Gracia stood and, from a package he had been carrying under his arm, removed the horn of a ram, the type that shepherds use. Don Pedro signaled to him.

"My eyes opened wide. I could not believe what they were about to do! Suddenly, Don Gabriel started to blow the horn. I started to shake, I screamed, and then, I must have fainted, for the next thing I knew, I was lying on a bed in Don Gabriel Gracia's mansion. Doctors hovered over me. Don Gabriel touched my shoulder compassionately. I lowered my eyes, embarrassed, for I recognized how much kindness he had shown me by saving my life, and how I had been ordered by the bishop to find evidence that would implicate him in the eyes of the Inquisition.

"Finally, Don Gabriel spoke, 'Last night we went out into the forest, as far as possible from the eyes and ears of the Inquisition. We went in order to sound the shofar in honor of Rosh Hashanah, in honor of our Father, Creator of the world. Even though we act as Christians, we are observant of as much of Judaism as possible under these conditions. We did not know that we had been followed until we heard your screams. We were frightened but decided to continue sounding the shofar the required number of times, knowing that we might be arrested, understanding that if we were to die, we wanted to die performing a *mitzvah*.

"'So we finished sounding the shofar, turned to go, and tripped over your fallen body. Don Pedro recognized you as the bishop's servant from the cloister. He was convinced that we should kill you in order to save ourselves. But I restrained him because there was something about you that was familiar. I suspected from the anguish I detected on your face that you were not in the cloister on your own free will, but perhaps you had been kidnapped. We carried you back to the carriage and to my house, and I called my personal physician, Don Luis, to attend to you. When he removed your clothes, it was my turn to scream. I had a son who had been kidnapped by the Church. He was very young at the time, and I thought I would never see him again. Besides being obvious that you are a Jewish man, you have a birthmark on your chest that I recognized. You are my son Yoseph.'

"Tears streamed down my cheeks as we embraced. For a long time, neither one of us could speak, but our eyes revealed the intensity of our pain. That night, we decided to flee from the lands of the Inquisition."

[We cannot positively ascertain that the family in this next story is the same Gracia family. However, the circumstances of their escape and the saga of how they rebuilt their lives are similar. Both stories are about games of hide and seek from the Inquisition.]

While still living in Lisbon, Beatrice de Luna (1510–1569) (Channa, Dona Gracia), daughter of the Nasi family, married Francisco (Tzemach) Mendez, son of the aristocratic, wealthy Benveniste family, also conversos, who were international bankers and gem merchants. Their only child Reyna (Malka) was born in 1530. Dona Gracia adopted two nephews, Joao Micas (Joseph) and Samuel, and raised them. Joseph later became her son-in-law and the public figure for the family business which she controlled from behind the scenes.

Widowed at the age of twenty-six, Dona Gracia plotted the family's escape from Portugal via England to Antwerp, succeeding in taking her wealth with her. Because there were many other conversos living there, she thought that she would be able to return openly to the observance of Judaism, which she loved and longed for with all her heart. But she was still not able to remove her Christian disguise and resume her life as a Jew because Emperor Charles V was envious of her great fortune and plotted to accuse her of being a heretic in order to confiscate all her property. It took her two years to satisfy the emperor through bribes and loans, and then she fled with her family to Venice where they thought they would be safe. But again this was not the case.

Meanwhile, nephew Joseph appealed to Sultan Suleiman, ruler of the Ottoman/Turkish Empire, to help in liberating the family from Christian Europe and to welcome them to his country. After eleven years of flight, Dona Gracia Mendez reached Constantinople and was able to return to the religion into which she was born.

Dona Gracia acquired a palace called Belvedere, located on the Bosphorus (Constantinople), and from there she directed her family's financial affairs. As difficult and dangerous as her disguise had been during her early life, so was her total commitment to Judaism once she reached safety. Belvedere became the center of Jewish affairs. She served dinner daily to eighty poor Jews. She organized and supported the *yeshiva* of Rabbi Joseph ibn Levy, as well as synagogues and other charitable institutions both in Constantinople and in Salonika. Through her connection with the good offices of the sultan, she aided in redemption of many other conversos, helping them resettle in countries not hostile to Jews so that they, too, could return to their faith. She was so successful in this endeavor that many of the Jews she helped were even able to transfer their property and their wealth to their new countries.

When the news reached her that Pope Paul IV had arrested the conversos who had been hiding in the Italian city of Ancona, with the purpose of turning them over to the Inquisition to be burned at the stake, she asked the sultan to put pressure on the Pope to release the Jews. The sultan hinted to the Pope that reprisals against Christians living in Constantinople would be made unless he ordered the release of the Jews he held prisoners. Then Dona Gracia organized a boycott of the port of Ancona and shifted her business to the port of Presaro. Eventually the Pope freed those Jews who were Turkish citizens who had been in Italy on business matters.

Dona Gracia's most important project was leasing the city of Tiberias (Eretz Yisrael) from the sultan for the sum of 1000 ducats a year for the purpose of rebuilding it as a home for the conversos who settled there after their escape. Plans were laid for a new defensive wall, a new bath at the hot springs, a printing press, and the creation of a textile center which would use the silk spun by silkworms and the wool of sheep grazing in the surrounding fields. These industries provided a livelihood for the many refugees who had returned "home."

By our standards, she was very young when she died, only fifty-nine years old. The news of La Senora's death was received all over the Jewish world with a profound sense of grief, for she had been truly a role model of kindness and love. The poet Samuel Usque compared her attributes to the illustrious women who preceded her, the compassion and piety of Miriam, the wisdom and governing ability of Deborah, the holiness and virtue of Esther. "The noble princess, the glory of Israel, the wise woman who built her house in holiness and purity, with her hand sustained the poor and needy...many are they whom she rescued from languishing in a dungeon ready for death...and led them into safe places. She founded houses where all may learn the law of God."

An Unusual Diary Entry:
A Conversation with Christopher Columbus

by

Menachem Mendel

This is an entry from the diary of Yosef ben HaLevi Haivri, (the Jew) known as Luis de Torres, written in Cuba, in the New World, on the land awarded to him by his majesty King Ferdinand of Spain, thirty-one years after Christopher Columbus discovered the Indies, on the occasion of his seventy-first birthday.[59]

I was born in Cordova, Andalusia, Spain. The details of how my people lived have already been recorded, both their illustrious contributions to this country during the Golden Age and the tremendous suffering imposed upon them after the Christian reconquest and the Inquisition. My father was a scribe who was privileged to write a Torah scroll during his lifetime. I was also educated to be a scribe, always surrounded by Hebrew books, manuscripts, and the Torah commentaries. I was fluent in the Hebrew language, and therefore I was invited to accompany Christopher Columbus as an interpreter on his voyage of discovery. He thought that when he would reach China and the Far East, he would locate the exiled Jews from the Ten Lost Tribes, and he wanted me to be able to communicate with them.

The three ships, the *Santa Maria*, the *Niña*, and the *Pinta*, sailed many days and nights until we sighted dry land. According to my calculations, we arrived on a Friday afternoon, two hours after mid-day, which on the Hebrew calendar was Hoshana Raba, twenty-one days in the month of Tishrei, in the year 5235 after creation. Because the memory of that day is so vivid in my mind, I am recording every detail as a chronicle for all future generations.

That fateful day, the day of our expulsion from Spain, was Tisha B'Av[60] on the Hebrew calendar in the year 5252/1492. That day had marked the tragedy of the destruction of both holy temples many centuries before, and now, one more tragic event was added to that mournful day. Three hundred thousand people, half the number redeemed from Egyptian slavery, descended to the Mediterranean Shore, searching for passage to a new land, to a land where they could openly practice Judaism. I was among them. However, I was not a refugee; I had been commissioned to join Christopher Columbus's voyage of discovery. I agreed to accompany him because I hoped that if we found Jewish brethren, I would be able to live my life in freedom and in peace. Don Rodriguez, his uncle Don Gabriel Sanchez, Alonso de Loquir, Rodrigo de Triana, Chon Kabrera, Doctor Birenal, and the Doctor Marko all agreed with my reasoning, and joined, but, except for Rodrigo, they sailed on the other ships. We were a large group of conversos, living in perpetual fear of Inquisition, hoping we could find a way out of the precarious situation we were in.

    We sailed for seventy-two days. Most of the time, the ocean was serene, and the trade winds blew gently from east to west. Usually, Columbus pored over the navigational diagrams that had been prepared for him by Rabbi Avraham Zacuto, an astronomer and historian who had fled from Spain to Portugal when the Jews were expelled. However, some of the time the ocean churned, heavy with storm, the waves blasting the sides of our ships, until we were sure they would capsize and we would all drown in the depths. On those frightful times, during the nights, Columbus stood on deck, his eyes searching for the occasional stars that darted in between the cumulonimbus clouds, watching for the appearance of the North Star to measure navigational latitude. He was determined to sail until he reached land, and his rallying call was, "*Adelante*! Sail on!"

    We sailed through the month of September, marking the holy days of Rosh Hashanah among ourselves. On the eve of Yom Kippur, which occurred on Sunday night that year, we saw a magnificent sight! Covered with lush, rich foliage, a sandbank floated in the middle of the ocean. We had had a backwards glimpse of the Canary Islands. It was our last sighting of land. The ocean was calm. Toward nightfall, I wrapped myself in my *talis*, went up on the deck, and chanted the "Kol Nidrei." Voices from the *Pinta* and the *Niña* echoed across the water and joined me in prayer. It seemed that the waves responded in rhythm to the sound of our voices.

When I finished the "Kol Nidrei," Columbus called me over to his side. "Isn't the dove one of the symbols of the Jewish people?" he queried. "You know that my family name, Colombo, also means 'dove.' There must be a reason for this voyage. We are not sailing on this ship in vain! Let me read to you what I have written here: 'And it came to pass on the day that the Jewish people were expelled from Spain at the hands of his majesty King Ferdinand. On that day the power was given to me to go forth to search new paths across this dark and fearsome ocean to an old world.'" We sat quietly, side by side, until the rays of the eastern light silvered the horizon.

Eleven days later, we noticed the first signs that land was not far distant. Sea swallows with long pointed wings and forked tails swooped gracefully overhead, plunging headlong into the water to catch small fish. I noticed that slender branches with leaves that were narrow, oval-shaped, tapering to a point, floated in the water and washed up near our ship. I was able to reach a branch, and when I pulled it from the water, I realized that I was holding a willow branch. I was overcome by joy. "It's a miracle, it's a miracle," I shouted. "In this new place, God had provided me with the willow branch so that I might fulfill the mitzvah of *Hoshana Raba*." I waved it enthusiastically toward the *Pinta*. Alonso de Loquir responded by waving his willow branch also.

That night, the night Hoshana Raba, all the sailors slept peacefully. The crescent of the moon sparked gloriously on the water while I sat all night with Rodrigo de Triana reciting *Tehillim* [Psalms], as is the custom on this night, from a Spanish translation. We read together by the light of the moon:

O give thanks unto the Lord, for He is good,
For His mercy endureth forever.
So let the redeemed of the Lord say,
Whom He has redeemed from the hand of the adversary. . . .
Then were they glad because they were quiet,
And He led them unto their desired haven.
          Tehillim 130:1, 2, 30

We beseech You, O Lord, save (us) now, Hoshana!
          Tehillim 118:29

With the first flickering light, we who had been awake all night were the first ones to see land. It was not a dream! It was not a vision! Rodrigo ran to alert Columbus that he had sighted land. The excitement and the hysterical screams awakened all the sailors on our ship and on the other two ships. They began to sing and dance to a new song: Land! Land! Land!

We disembarked on the beach at Fernandez Bay, San Salvador, and took possession of a New World for Spain. Columbus always believed that this island and the other ones he sighted later on this voyage of discovery were the Indies, near Japan or China.

And I, Yosef ben HaLevi Haivri, sang with my friends, with Alonso de Loquir, Chon Kabrera, Rodrigo de Triana, Don Rodriguez, Don Gabriel Sanchez, Doctor Birenal, and Doctor Marko a different song, a song of thanksgiving to God for leading us to a place where we might publicly acknowledge our Judaism.

BLESSINGS FOR THE DAYS OF AWE[61]

Candle Blessing

(Saypol, *My Very Own Rosh Hashanah Book*, pp. 26–27)

Kaddish – Blessing over the Wine/Juice

Traditional

Hamotzi – Blessing over the Bread

(Saypol, *My Very Own Rosh Hashanah Book*, p. 26)

Tapuchim Ud'Vash
Apples and Honey [62]

Ap - ples and hon - ey for Rosh Ha - sha - nah
Ap - ples and hon - ey for Rosh Ha - sha - nah A
good new year, A sweet new year!
Ap - ples and hon - ey for Rosh Ha - sha - nah

(Saypol, *My Very Own Rosh Hashanah Book*, p. 31)

Vahakimoti Et B'riti
(Genesis 17: 7.9)

Music: M. Rothblum
Arrangement: G. Fogelman

Va - ha - ki - mo - ti et b'ri - ti, va - ha - ki - mo - ti et b'ri - ti,
va - ha - ki - mo - ti et b'ri - ti bei - ni u - vei - ne - cha. Va -
yo - mer E - lo - him el Av - ra - ham et b'ri - ti tish' -
more, va - yo - mer E - lo - him el Av - ra - ham et b'ri - ti tish' - mor

"And I will Maintain My covenant between Me and you.
And God said to Abraham, 'You shall keep my Covenant.'"

(Friedman, *Sounds of Creation*, p. 11)

L'Shanah Tovah [63]

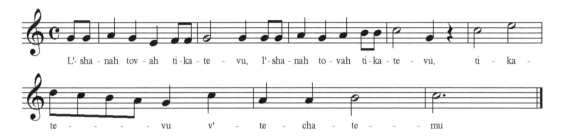

(Saypol, *My Very Own Rosh Hashanah Book*, pp. 26–27)

So Many Years Ago

S.H. Adler

The first day God made light, called Day;
He made the darkness, Night.
The second day God made the sky;
It was the heaven bright.

The third day God made land, called earth.
God made the oceans soon.
The fourth day lights to fill the sky,
He made the sun and moon.

The fifth day God made fish that swim,
The bird, the fowl, the bee.
The sixth day creatures of the earth,
Adam and Eve made He.

The seventh day God's work was done;
He rested in His way.
God made it holy for our prayers,
So we have Sabbath Day.

(Coopersmith, *The New Jewish Songbook*, p. 156)

Sing Along Song [64]

by

Steve Reuben

Rosh Hashanah celebrates
The birthday of the world,
Apples and honey to sweeten the year
Of ev'ry girl and boy.
      (chorus)

Rosh Hashanah starts the year.
Hear the shofar blow,
Telling us that we should act
The best way that we know.
      (chorus)

Yom Kippur reminds us that
It is atonement day.
We are sorry for the thoughtless
Things we often say.
      (chorus)

Yom Kippur's a time when we
Can begin once again.
Go to someone we have hurt
And say, "Come, let's be friends."
      (chorus)

(Reuben, *Especially Wonderful Days*, p. 4)

Chanukah

As winter approaches the days are darker, colder and shorter. On the twenty-fifth day of *Kislev*, the Jewish people begin the celebration of *Chanukah*. The month of Kislev is the third month in the Hebrew calendar and overlaps with November and/or December in the solar calendar. Chanukah is a minor holiday within the cycle of the year, a holiday having its origin in history rather than the Torah. However minor it is for the rabbis, Chanukah has become the most widely celebrated holiday in Jewish households. Looking more closely at Chanukah we see that it is a holiday open to many interpretations. Just as the play cloth gets imbued with meaning through the imagination of the young child, Chanukah has the potential to evolve from a minor holiday into a more fully realized spiritual celebration based on how one chooses to "play" with it.

If the teacher is unfamiliar with the Chanukah story, she should begin by reading the version included in the eighth grade section. There are two key elements in understanding Chanukah. The first element is the preserved story of a military victory. The second element is the miracle of light.

Let us look first at the story, which takes place around 167 B.C.E. At that time, the Syrian King Antiochus ruled the lands of the Jewish people. He declared himself a godhead and went about his kingdom forcing people to worship altars to himself and the Greek gods. In addition, Antiochus did not allow the Jews to celebrate Shabbat or any other festivals, nor could they circumcise their children. The issue of circumcision was very divisive. Rabbi Shira Milgrom elaborates that on the one hand there were the Jews who considered circumcision the very essence of their covenant with God. On the other hand there were the Greeks who worshipped the body as the most holy temple and saw the act of circumcision as a defiling of that temple. In other periods of their history, Jews were able to feign conversion while still practicing secretly. Because the body was often fully exposed during the Greek period, the Jews could not hide this most sacred symbol of their religion. They had no choice but to either Hellenize or defy Antiochus's decree and remain fully practicing Jews.[65]

The Jews in the larger cities tended to assimilate faster than the Jews in the country, which is a trend also in present times. The story of Chanukah takes place in Mod'in, a small town, which was not as strongly influenced by Greek culture. When the Hebrew priest Mattathias saw another Jew bowing down to the idol of Antiochus, he struck the Jew down, killing him and inciting the Syrian army to retaliate. This priest was not aware of the increasing numbers of Hellenized Jews in the population. He was not yet jaded, as were the other priests in the larger cities. Mattathias was able to rouse his small community, especially his own family, and convince them that staying true to themselves was worth any struggle. Mattathias's son, Judah Maccabee, led the resistance. The Maccabees, or "hammers," struck down the Syrian armies through cunning and familiarity with their home terrain. After defeating the armies, the Maccabees set to restoring their temple, which had been profaned during the battle.

Let us examine this much of the story and how it relates to the Waldorf school. In some ways, the Jewish families in the Waldorf schools are both the Maccabees and the Hellenized Jews. They have consciously chosen to send their children to a school whose festivals are predominately Christian but whose pedagogy offers the children experiences of beauty, harmony, cultural awareness and ways of thinking that are not found in other school systems. The parents swing between enchantment with the school and frustration that their own culture may not be adequately represented. The Jewish families then begin asking for more acknowledgement by the school and some begin to take on the spirit of the Maccabee, "hammering" away at the school until they feel represented and acknowledged. The faculty then must ask themselves, "Do we treat these families the same as all the others? After all, they have chosen to be here (they have Hellenized themselves). Or can we honor their struggle for 'religious freedom' within this community?"

Chanukah can be a vehicle for reconciliation between the Jewish families and the school. Acknowledging that Chanukah is a celebration of the triumph of religious freedom, the school can use the days of Chanukah as a time to dialogue with the Jewish families. Remember too, that the original fighting in the Chanukah story was between Jews. The whole issue of inclusion in the school might be a very volatile one within the Jewish population. Some families might look down upon others for completely "Hellenizing," and others for stirring up trouble. In the end, the health of the social organism of the school depends upon the expansion of this dialogue within the parent body as well as within the College. If the school has a Chanukah celebration, or even a parent study night, this can serve to bring families and faculty together once a year. It is a way for the school to say, "We honor who you are."

The military story of Chanukah is rather straightforward. Let us look at the miracle of light and the other symbols of Chanukah that speak to the Waldorf school. After their military victory, the Maccabees set about cleansing their defiled temple. Then they needed to rededicate it, and to do this they needed to light the *Ner Tamid*, the everlasting light. Amidst the rubble, a single cruse of oil was found, enough for only one day. The Maccabees lit the Ner Tamid and miraculously the light burned for eight days. In the Book of Maccabees the light was not originally recorded as a miracle. Only later did the rabbis emphasize the story of light over the story of military power. By doing this, they emphasized again God's influence in Jewish history rather than people carrying out important events on their own. To contrast the military story, the story of Zechariah is read on Chanukah. In Zechariah 4: 1–7, God speaks through an angel saying: "Not by might and not by power but by My spirit alone shall we all live in peace." Here is the root of Jewish pacifism.

In *Eight Lights, Eight Nights*, Rabbi Avi Weiss says that the true miracle of Chanukah is that, knowing there was so little oil, the Maccabees attempted to light the lamp at all.[66] During Chanukah the teacher can reflect upon times when her students have made attempts at something even when they knew there was potential for failure. Those are moments full of courage. Were they acknowledged silently or openly? Reflecting on these moments of courage could inspire the teacher's writing of holiday verses for individual children.

Chanukah means "rededication." As the dark days begin and the school readies itself for winter break, the teacher can view the eight days of Chanukah as a time for re-dedication. The teacher can approach each new candle with a personal meditation. "How can I rededicate myself to the class, the parents, the faculty, the college, the community, the greater community, my family, myself?" In this way, even a teacher unfamiliar with Jewish traditions can see the ritual of Chanukah as personally meaningful.

The lighting of the *menorah* is the way in which Jewish families re-member the miracle of light. In the menorah there are places for eight candles all in a row. A ninth candle, the *shammash*, or "servant," stands apart—higher, lower, or parallel to the other candles, while still being part of the menorah. This is a clear metaphor for the role of the teacher in the Waldorf school. The teacher is the shammash, servant and guide, throughout eight years with a class. She is part of the whole, yet also stands apart. When a teacher lights the menorah, she can "rededicate" herself as shammash to the children. The candle for the newest day is always lit first, then lighting the previous days' candles follows. This too is symbolic for the Waldorf teacher. She and her class may be living in the present grade, but the previous years remain illuminated as well, each year building upon the last. Imagine the inner spirit of the eighth grader shining as brilliantly as the menorah does on the eighth night. If the teachers have truly been shammashes, it will be so. A similar picture is offered by Carlos Pietzner in *Festival Images for Today*. He suggests that by taking on the warmth and light of the candles we become vehicles for the light of Christ.[67]

Advent and Chanukah share the images of light and darkness. The start of Chanukah was chosen so that the new moon would occur during the festival week. Chanukah can be experienced as both earthly journey and personal journey into the folds of darkness and then emerging into light once again. The menorah is built upon this metaphor, beginning already at the place of darkness. On the first night there is but one candle blazing in the darkness. Throughout a week and a day the light builds, a gradual kindling of the brilliance that eventually illuminates the home and the spirit. There is singing, game playing and storytelling. The lights of Chanukah burn down while families reconnect with each other. This holiday, like Christmas, is family-centered.

So why do Jewish families sometimes feel alienated in the wintertime? Once again it seems like there are simple steps that can be taken to bridge the gap during the winter festivals. Some schools have chosen to rename the Advent spiral as the "Winter Spiral" or the "Spiral of Light." While the spiral presents a similar image of entering the darkness and bringing light, many Jewish families still feel uneasy. For some, the plethora of Christmas songs as part of the ritual may be what decides involvement. Certainly Advent is about the coming of Christ, and the school can choose to imbue the spiral with that meaning alone. If, however, they wish for all the children to have an experience that speaks to them, the school might consider some alternatives. Carlos Pietzner recounts an Advent spiral where each child was allowed to pick the song that would be sung during her walk through the spiral.[68] Given a choice, the Jewish children might pick songs that had special meaning to them and still allowed them the experience of the spiral.

Chanukah has become an important holiday primarily in response to Christmas. Jewish children "needed" a winter festival of their own. This is somewhat ironic considering how the story of Chanukah emphasizes loyalty and separation rather than assimilation. Chanukah and Christmas both have in common a loss of their true meaning within the current societal norms of celebration. Both holidays have been commercialized and many families celebrate them not because they want to but because they are obliged to. The Waldorf schools have done a great deal of parent education around Advent and Christmas. They have helped many families simplify the gift-giving aspect and bring new meaning to the season. The schools could help the Jewish parents likewise.

In some situations a more thoughtful use of language would broaden the scope of the activity and help all parents feel acknowledged and included, rather than inadvertently perpetuate feelings of exclusion. For example, one Waldorf school set aside a Saturday in November for the parents to come together and learn simple crafts, which they could give as gifts for their children. This was a wonderful idea and helped many parents with an alternative to the commercial aspect of Christmas. This day was called "Heart of Advent," which could be easily construed to imply that the crafts were solely for Christian holidays. An alternative title for the event would have not only set a more appropriate tone but been more inclusive of the Jewish families who came to participate, thereby enriching the community experience for everyone.

Unlike Michaelmas and the Days of Awe, Chanukah and Christmas overlap in season but not entirely in spirit. While there is a lot of meaning in Chanukah that can speak directly to the teacher, she should not force an artificial overlap between Christmas and Chanukah. Rather, in keeping with the essence of Chanukah, the festival should be acknowledged in its own right. The Christ-Being's message is love, compassion, and goodwill towards all. In itself this offers an opportunity for the school to live into the essence of the Christmas season by making sure they are extending their consciousness to the diverse members of the school community.

Faculty Verse

A Meditation for Chanukah

"When God began to create the heaven and the earth—the earth being unformed and void, with darkness over the surface of the deep and a wind from God sweeping over the surface of the deep and a wind from God sweeping over the water—God said 'Let there be light': and there was light." Genesis 1:1–3

>Amidst darkness veiling darkness
>a small flame flickers in the night
>The first one is hardest to light
>The shammash, the server, first glimmer against the enveloping night
>When the darkness of isolation is momentarily faced, seen, and slowly approached.
>One candle against the darkness
>In the blackest time of the year
>Scarcely a bonfire makes.
>Yet this is the shammash, the server,
>The one which will light the others.
>Tradition holds that this candle,
>the candle of dedication,
>is *or haganuz*, the hidden light
>which gives off more strength than light,
>Strength to seek out the inner soul righteousness
>of faith, of dedication,
>and stir it awake.
>Even on the first night, this light kindles another.
>This light finds a companion of the spirit.
>This light serves eternity,
>a pinprick of reminder to do the good deed promised but undone,
>a glow of memory to act in the name of one loved and lost,
>a probe to find courage to speak truth where there was silence.
>This light serves righteousness.

Slowly, night by night, candle by candle,
holiness increases,
courage increases,
righteousness increases,
until darkness is aglow with hope,
with righteous deeds, with memories kindling
another,
Night by night,
Until the cloak of despair is shed in promise
Night by night, the server serves holy light.

The miracle of lights burning is the rededication
of souls
from despair to promise,
from darkness to light,
from doubt to completion.

We are commanded to light these lights,
commanded to strike against emptiness,
commanded to hope,
commanded amidst darkness veiling darkness
to make a server of the divine light.

"Blessed are You, Lord our God, Ruler of the world,
Who makes us holy
through divine commandments and commands us to
light candles of dedications."

– Author Unknown[69]

Symbols and Traditions of Chanukah

The lighting of the menorah (or *chanukkiah*) is the primary tradition for this holiday. The menorah has places for nine candles, eight for the eight days of the miracle of the oil and one for the shammash. Shammash means "servant," and it is the shammash which lights all the other candles. This tradition came in part because the rabbis decided that the lights of the chanukkiah could not be used for any work. This created a dilemma, for if the candles could not be "functional" in a practical sense, how could the rest of the candles be lit if the first could not do the lighting? Thus the shammash was added to the menorah to serve as the lighting candle. Since no work is supposed to be done using the lights of the menorah, any work that is carried out, such as reading, playing dreidel, or opening presents, is done by the light of the shammash.

The candles are placed into the menorah from right to left. Then they are lit from left to right, so that the newest day's candle is always burning first. The shammash is lit first, the blessings are recited, and then the rest of the candles are lit. Many people sing songs after lighting the candles, the most traditional of which is "*Mo'oz Tsur*, Rock of Ages." To bring more reflection into this holiday, some families attribute a different theme to each evening. In the book *Eight Nights, Eight Lights* by Rabbi Kerry Olizky, the themes of courage, gratitude, sharing, knowledge, service, understanding, love and hope are attributed to each candle and used as points of departure for discussion and sharing.

Gelt (money) was given to children to reward them for Torah study, for during Chanukah the Torah is supposed to be read all eight nights. This tradition slowly transformed into the exchanging of presents, primarily in response to the gift-giving tradition of Christmas. It would be interesting to return to the original intent for gelt, the focus on study. Unfortunately, for most Jews these days, gift-giving at Chanukah occurs because it is expected, not because it has been earned. The teacher can encourage her Jewish and Christian families alike to look for gifts that speak to what the child has been doing in school. Giving books, models, handwork kits, or new colored pencils can tie the school life into the Jewish family experience.

Playing with the spinning top, *dreidel*, is also a popular Chanukah tradition. While gambling is usually frowned upon in Judaism, dreidel is an exception. It is told that during the time of the Maccabees, when children went to study Torah in groups, they would bring a dreidel with them. One child would be a lookout and when a Syrian soldier approached, they would signal the others. The other children would quickly hide their books and bring out the dreidel, appearing to be playing rather than studying.[70]

The dreidel has four Hebrew letters on it; *nun*, *gimmel*, *heh* and *shin*. These are the first letters in the saying, "*Nes Gadol Hayah Sham* (A great miracle happened there)." To play dreidel a class divides into groups of three or four children. For ante, the teacher may want to provide a treat, such as nuts, that the children can later eat, or the children can use their counting stones from math. The game begins as each child puts the same amount of tokens from his or her pile into the communal pot. The teacher should decide who begins in each group, such as the youngest or the oldest. The first player spins the dreidel and does whatever the dreidel "says" to do. When a *nun* faces up, the player does nothing. When a *gimmel* faces up, the player takes the whole pot. When a *heh* faces up, the player takes half the pot. When a *shin* faces up, the player puts one into the pot. When the pot is empty, everyone puts two tokens back in and the game begins again. The play continues until someone has won all of the other children's tokens or time is up. I have seen kindergarten children happily spinning the dreidel as well as older children; it is a truly multi-generational game!

Oily food is eaten on Chanukah to remind us of the miracle of the burning oil. The most traditional food of Chanukah is latkes, or potato pancakes. Even in our health-conscious times, it is hard to resist a crispy on the outside, tender on the inside, oil-laden latke. Latkes are usually topped with sour cream, applesauce, or both. When our school was smaller, the Jewish parents in the school would gather in the kitchen and make plates of latkes for all the classes. It was a wonderful opportunity for the parents to share their family traditions with each other and with the children. As the school grew, this tradition changed and now the third grade children and parents prepare the latkes for the school. If there are no families with their own recipes for latkes, an abundance of recipes can be found in Jewish holiday books or on the Internet.

One final note about Chanukah: Throughout this curriculum guide the teacher will find many spelling variations for the name of this holiday. Chanukkah, Channukah, Hanukah, and Hanuka are all acceptable, though the most common spellings are Chanukah and Hanukkah. The teacher could choose the one that is easiest for her to spell consistently, or the faculty could agree on which version the school will use.

Blessings for Chanukah Candles

Baruch atah Adonai Eloheynu melech ha'olam, asher kid'shanu b'mitzvotav v'tzivanu l'hadleek ner shel Hanukah.

Blessed be You, Lord our King, Ruler of the Universe, Who makes us holy through His commandments and commands us to light the Hanukah candles.[71]

or

Blessed are You, Adonai, Eternal One, Who enables us to welcome Hanukah by kindling these lights.[72]

Baruch atah Adonai Eloheynu melech ha'olam, sheh-asah nisseem l'avotenu ba-yamim ha'heym bazman hazeh.

Blessed be You, Lord our King, Ruler of the Universe, Who worked miracles for our ancestors in those days at this very season.[73]

    The following is a new blessing for the Chanukah candles written by a contemporary Jewish feminist liturgist, Marcia Falk. She wrote, "I think it's important that children learn that liturgy is created by real people, not just handed down from the mountain of tradition. Who knows? They may be inspired by this to write their own blessings."[74]

    Hadlakat Neyrot Hanukah
        Yitromeym libeynu,
        t'shovav nafsheynu,
        b'hadlakat neyrot shel Hanukah.

    Hanukah Candlelighting
        May our hearts be lifted,
        our spirits refreshed,
        as we light the Hanukah candles.
                  — Marcia Falk[75]

Chanukah in the First Grade

The first graders' experience of Chanukah can be an introduction to the rituals of the festival. The dark days of winter have arrived and the first graders, still resonant with the sense of beauty and gratitude provided in kindergarten, can experience Chanukah as the "festival of lights." Both stories provided here focus on the candles of the menorah.

"Bee-utiful Candles" is a pixie-tale that culminates in the making of candles. The teacher could tell the story "Bee-utiful Candles" the day before Chanukah and then the class could make rolled beeswax candles as an activity the following day.[76] The menorah needs forty-four candles. Depending on the size of the class, each child could make one or two candles that would then be used in the classroom menorah. Another possibility would be for the parents to make the candles at a parent evening. During this activity the parents could meditate on their child and what they would like to "illuminate" in their child's soul. The eight days of Chanukah candlelight could then carry the children through the darkness in a manner similar to the way a faculty carries a child during child study.

A story that is highly recommended, but not included in this anthology, is "The Devil's Trick," written by Isaac Bashevis Singer, in which the light of the menorah helps a young child triumph over a devil character. This story carries the inner dimension of Chanukah to the children: light prevailing over darkness. It also sets a tone for reverence, as the devil learns that "Chanukah is no time for making trouble." This saying might be helpful during the period of heightened anticipation that often accompanies the holiday season.

The class teacher may wish to invite Jewish parents into the class to begin the lighting of the candles. The class would then hear the Hebrew blessings and watch the ritual as done by someone for whom this is part of their yearly practice. This would help the non-Jewish children experience Chanukah less as a concept and more as a living picture. This is especially true for teachers who wish to acknowledge Chanukah but have no Jewish families in their own class.

The first graders can also revel in the image of the dreidel. The dreidel verses are full of activity and lend themselves to circle time quite effortlessly. If the first grade teacher is apprehensive about the "gambling" in traditional dreidel, there are other alternatives. The class could have a dreidel race instead. The class breaks up into groups as in regular dreidel, but in this game they try to see who can make the dreidel spin the longest. The group would need to be given a standard of time measurement, such as "one-banana, two-banana," which they would say aloud as the dreidel spins. The longest spinners from each group could then have a final spin-off. This form of dreidel playing can be seen as a dormant seed for the physics curriculum of the upper grades. Observe how these first grade children come up with ideas for making the dreidel spin longer. Mechanics in action!

The image of the menorah lends itself to a first grade form drawing:

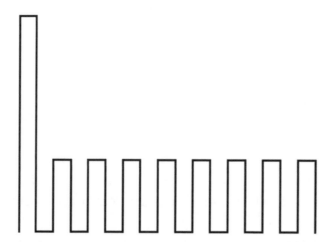

This can be done on one day and then the next day the children can fill in the rest of the picture by adding a base and candles.

The most popular Chanukah songs for younger children are "My Dreidel," "Oh Hanukah," and "Hanukah." "Chag Ha-Or" is lesser known, but also quite appropriate for first grade. In first grade the teacher might wish to sing the song an octave higher than it is written. In discussing the songs with our school music teacher, who is both a class teacher and an anthroposophic music therapist, she encouraged me to remind teachers that the folk songs of different peoples speak to the children in a unique way, and out of this stream it is acceptable to sing non-pentatonic songs in the early grades.[77] If, however, the teacher wishes to stay the course of the pentatonic mood, one could sing an octave higher and transpose the F#, which would make the song in the mood of the fifth. The song "Kindle the Taper" can also easily be transposed into the mood of the fifth. The first verse carries the image of the light and candle and relates it to the heavenly stars, again bridging the imagery from the Christmas and Chanukah festivals.

Verses for First Grade

DREIDEL SONG
    Twirl about, dance about,
    Spin, spin, spin!
    Turn, Dreidel, turn—
    Time to begin!

    Soon it is Hanukkah—
    Fast, Dreidel, fast!
    For you will lie still
    When Hanukkah's past.
        – Efraim Rosenzweig[78]

Spin, Little Dreidels
>Spin, little dreidels, go, go, go. (turn)
>Spin, little dreidels, now, go slow. (turn slowly)
>Spin, little dreidels, jump so high. (jump)
>Spin, little dreidels, reach for the sky. (stretch arms upward)
>Spin, little dreidels, touch your nose. (touch nose)
>Spin, little dreidels, stand on your toes. (stand on toes)
>Spin, little dreidels, take a hop. (hop on one foot)
>Spin, little dreidels, don't you stop. (keep hopping)
>Spin, little dreidels, spin around. (turn)
>Spin, little dreidels, drop to the ground. (sit)
>> – Sylvia Rouss[79]

Five Little Latkes in the Frying Pan
>Five little latkes in the frying pan.
>I'd like to eat them if I can.
>The first one said, "I'm frying in oil."
>The second one said, "I've been placed in foil."
>The third one said, "I'm very good to eat."
>The fourth one said, "I'm a Chanukah treat."
>The fifth one said, "I know you'll like me.
>Take a bite, and you will see."
>> – Sylvia Rouss[80]

So Many Candles
>There are so many candles,
>Standing straight and tall.
>Help me count them.
>Let us count them all:
>1, 2, 3, 4, 5, 6, 7, 8.
>You are doing fine.
>Count the shammash.
>That makes nine.
>> – Sylvia Rouss[81]

Bee-utiful Candles[82]

by

Leonard Jaffe

The Pitzel-sailors had forgotten to get Hanukkah candles the last time they sailed over the Star of David Lake, and now, with Hanukkah only one day away, there was not a single Hanukkah candle anywhere in Pitzel-land! Oh, there were plenty of dreidels and there would be stacks and stacks of potato latkes, but whoever heard of Hanukkah without Hanukkah candles?

All the Pitzels were sad, of course, but saddest of all were the children. They could hardly eat breakfast that morning, and when they left their snug little houses under the strawberry bushes, they couldn't think of playing. In fact, all David and his sister Sarah and their friends could think of doing was to sit in the shade of some violets and poke the ground with their feet!

A hummingbird was watching them. He didn't know why they were sad, but he didn't care. "Pitzel children should always be laughing," he said to himself, "and in a minute they will be!" Then he darted over and began flying around their heads—backwards. Debbie, Sol, and Harvey did laugh at this trick, and some of the others smiled. But when the hummingbird stopped and hung perfectly still, right there in midair, all the Pitzels laughed out loud, except one, because David wasn't laughing. He wasn't even smiling. He was listening.

Suddenly David jumped up—the hummingbird's hum had reminded him of something! "Bees!" he shouted. "And bees make wax, don't they, hummingbird?"

"All the time," answered the hummingbird.

"Then we're saved!" David cried. "We can get wax from the bees and make our own Hanukkah candles!"

"Not so fast!" said the hummingbird. "If you want wax from bees, you'll have to ask the queen for it, and from what I've heard about her, you'll never get it!"

"Anyway, we've got to try—it's our only chance!" said David. "What's the queen's name hummingbird? I'll ask her myself. I'm not afraid!"

"Let's see, I knew her name once...Mel—lifica; yes, that's it—Queen Mellifica!"

All right, Queen Mellifica—here I come!" David announced, bravely throwing out his chest.

But Sarah could tell David didn't feel at all brave. "Wait for me!" she called after him as he started off. And hand in hand, brother and sister walked down the path to the hollow tree where the bees lived.

Now, Queen Mellifica really wasn't a bad queen, no matter what the hummingbird had heard. But she did have her "bad days," and, unluckily for David and Sarah, this was one of them. And so when the Lord of the Queenbee Chamber came to tell her that two Pitzels were outside the hive wanting to see her, she almost flew off her couch, crying out, "Impossible, impossible! You know very well, Lord Apis, that today is one of my bad days! I'm in no condition to see anyone, and certainly not Pitzels, whoever they are. Send them away!"

"Forgive me, Your Majesty," Lord Apis quietly answered, "but I think you should see them. You need a little cheering up, and the Pitzels are—well, they're funny! You never leave the hive, of course, and so you cannot know what funny creatures there are in this world!"

"Funny? In what way are the Pitzels funny?"

"Well, first of all," Lord Apis went on, "they have no wings—they have to walk all the time! As if that weren't enough, the poor things have only four legs, instead of six! But the funniest part of all is, they walk on only two of their legs, while the other two just hang—just hang!"

"Enough!" laughed the queen. "If what you say is true, have them brought to me immediately!"

Lord Apis hurried to the entrance of the hive to tell David and Sarah that the queen had graciously consented to see them. Then he ordered one of the drone bees to fly them up to the throne room.

David and Sarah mounted on the drone's back and up they went, breathing in the soft, sweet smell of the honey and passing row after row of bee cells, each waxen row glowing with a different color. At last they reached the highest point of the hive, the throne room itself, shining in a blaze of gold!

Standing now in the presence of the queen, David made a real bow, while Sarah curtsied to the floor. They stayed that way, waiting for the queen to speak. But it took some time for the queen to speak. The Pitzels seemed even funnier to her than Lord Apis had described them.

Finally, she controlled herself and said, "Why have you come? Tell me quickly, for I must get my rest. Yesterday, you see, I laid 4,281 eggs! You might tell that to your queen, by the way—4,281 eggs in one day!"

"We Pitzels have no queen," Sarah said in a whisper.

"What? No queen, no queen! Now I understand why you go around like that, on only two of your legs! Anything can happen without a queen! Oh, well, come to the point—what is it you want?

David cleared his throat. "Wax, Your Majesty. We Pitzels need wax."

"Wax?! Whatever for? I can see you don't live in a hive, so why would you need wax?"

"For candles," David replied.

"And what are candles?" the queen asked. "What do you do with them?

"Burn them, Your Majesty."

"Burn them? Then what is left of the wax?"

"Why...nothing!" David said.

"Nothing?" Queen Mellifica could hardly believe what she was hearing. "You mean you'll take my good wax and make it into things called candles only in order to burn them up until there's nothing left? In other words, you want my wax—for nothing!...Well, this must be some kind of Pitzel joke, and I suppose it all comes again from not having a queen to guide you, but I assure you, we are not amused! I bid you good day!"

"Oh, please, Your Majesty," David cried out. "We do want your wax for something, something very important. You don't understand about candles. You see, when the sun goes down tomorrow, we Pitzels start celebrating our holiday of Hanukkah. Hanukkah is a wonderful, a beautiful holiday—but only if there are candles. Hanukkah is even called the Feast of Lights! It lasts for eight days, and each day we light one more candle until, on the last day, the special candlestick is full. And while the candles burn and their flames dance in the air, they makes us think of the time when our freedom and our Temple were won back for us by the good, the brave, the magnificent Maccabees—"

"Macca-bees, macca-bees?" interrupted the queen. "I've never heard of those bees before, though I dare say they're distant relatives of ours—we are honeybees, you know. . . . Well now, that's a completely different story! If those candles of yours make you think of bees—macca or any other kind—they are important for you to have! In that case, you're welcome to the wax!"

David and Sarah began shouting, "Thank you, thank you!" but the queen quieted them. "Please, please, I have a head-buzz as it is! Now then, my workers will spend the rest of the day filling up on honey and they'll be ready with your wax tomorrow morning. Where shall I send them?"

"To the Star of David Lake, Your Majesty." David said. "Uncle Ben has his workshop there. He's a sculptor. He'll know how to make your wax into candles."

Queen Mellifica nodded. Then slowly, with great dignity, she rose up from her throne and began flying out of the room. Just before she left, however, she said to herself—loud enough for David and Sarah to hear, "The macca-bees may well have been as brave as those Pitzels say. But I wonder if their queen ever laid 4,281 eggs in a single day!" David and Sarah giggled as they ran back down out of the hive.

Outside, their friends were waiting, and when David and Sarah told them what had happened, they all raced home to spread the wonderful news.

Soon Pitzel-land looked like a carnival. Mother and father Pitzels, grandmother and grandfather Pitzels, and aunt and uncle Pitzels sang and danced with the children in the streets. And up in the air they tossed their heroes, David and Sarah, again and again and again!

The celebration did not last very long, though, because Uncle Ben climbed up on a mushroom and, using a morning glory as a loudspeaker, called out, "Fellow Pitzels—your attention, please! If we want to be ready for the bees tomorrow morning, we must start making the candle molds right away!"

The Pitzels realized Uncle Ben was right. Without another word they followed him to the lake. There, they began rolling up bits of clay and covering them with the plaster Uncle Ben was mixing in the meantime. They worked and worked, and it was night before they were finished.

What a sight all those plaster casts made in the moonlight—it looked as though the shore were covered with a forest of tiny white trees!

"You can go home now," Uncle Ben told them. "When the plaster is dry, the clay will have to be taken out, and that's a job only I can do with my special tools. But I could use one person to help me."

"Let me!" David cried, and before his mother had time to say no, all the other Pitzels shouted: "Yes, David! Let David!" So David stayed up that whole night helping Uncle Ben remove the clay from the insides of the molds.

The sun was just stretching over the edge of the sky when the Pitzels gathered on the shore again. No one spoke. Everyone was thinking about the same thing—the candle molds are ready, yes, but would Queen Mellifica keep her promise?

Then a strange thing happened. Although by now the sun had fully risen, it suddenly got very dark. The Pitzels looked up—it was the bees coming toward them, covering the sky in a huge swarm! The Pitzels cheered. With Lord Apis in front, the bees landed in a most orderly fashion.

"Do you think each of your workers could fill a hole like this with his wax?" Uncle Ben asked, holding up a mold in front of Lord Apis.

Lord Apis smiled. "Any one of my workers could fill ten of those holes!" Then he buzzed out a command.

The bees quickly scattered, each of them settling on top of a mold and letting his wax drip down into the hole. As soon as a bee was finished, a Pitzel ran up and pushed a piece of thread through the center of the wax. The thread was for the candlewick, of course.

"We must be off now," said Lord Apis, when all the holes had been filled with wax and all the candlewicks were in place. "We were glad to help you, but it is rather a shame you couldn't have done such a simple thing yourselves. However, we can't all be bees!"

"That's right," smiled Uncle Ben, and the Pitzels waved until the bees were out of sight.

"My friends," said Uncle Ben, "when you're quite sure the wax is hard, you may break open the plaster shells and take out your Hanukkah candles! As for me, I'm going to get some sleep now, and David should do the same!"

"He certainly should," said David's mother. "But look, he's asleep already!"

And so he was, right there on the shore, with his arms tight around one of the candle molds. He was still hugging the mold when his father carried him home and put him to bed.

David slept until the smell of potato latkes woke him up. Rubbing his eyes, he walked into the dining room. "Happy Hanukkah!" cried his mother and father, grandmother and grandfather, and Sarah and Uncle Ben.

In the middle of the holiday table was the menorah with the first candle in it, a gay orange-colored one.

"David, you will light the menorah tonight," his father said, "and for a shammash you can use the candle in that mold you're holding."

David looked down at this hand—he hadn't even realized he was holding a mold. He quickly broke it open. Inside was a candle as golden as Queen Mellifica's throne room itself!

David lit the shammash, and with it, the first candle. And, at the same time, the very same thing was happening in every other house in Pitzel-land!

Chanukah in the Second Grade

The first grade experience of Chanukah comes and goes without a direct exposure to the official story of Chanukah. Now in second grade, the children can be exposed to the story, perhaps at a winter assembly where the story of Chanukah is told. The whole story may enter the children's consciousness, but the teacher should return to the classroom and emphasize the miracle of the oil. The light of God that helped the Maccabees is harmonious with the light of the Christ-being who helps the Saints in the second grade curriculum.

The story of Deborah has the tenor of a saint story, in that she opens herself up to a divine light that later allows her to help her people. In this story Deborah is a young girl, perhaps not much older than the second graders. Since many of the saints stories are about men, this story may speak more directly to the girls in the class. It is also a pedagogical story responding to the emerging cattiness of eight-year-olds. Deborah's mantra translates as: "How good it is for people to live in peace," which speaks to both classmate dynamics and the greater themes of the season and the second grade year. The verse, "Eight Are the Lights" is also a reflection of the second grade themes that are embodied through the saints stories.

The second graders may be familiar with the plot of "One Hanukkah in Helm." It is a Jewish version of the stone soup folk story that might have been told in kindergarten or first grade. For second grade more background to the story can be told, with the town turning away both from beggars and from each other. The elements of charity combined with a communal spirit again reflect the work of second grade.

The second graders can be led on a Chanukah number journey related to the menorah. Chanukah begins with two candles, the next night there are three and so on. The number journey would be 2+3+4+5+6+7+8+9, which gives the total number of candles needed for the menorah. This also plants a seed for algebraic exponents in the upper grades. For another math game, refer to the third grade section.

Riddles are also part of the Chanukah celebration, and the second graders might enjoy being "challenged" after the candles are lit. The following riddles are from the book *Jewish Holiday Fun*: [83]

What time is it when you sit on a burning candle?
Springtime.

How can you light a Chanukah candle without a match?
Take a candle out of the box and the box will be a candle lighter.

Why won't the old candle maker make candles any longer?
Because the candles are long enough.

The teacher can find more riddles by asking for family favorites from the parent body or by making them up herself. There might even be an older class that would like to try their hand at writing riddles for the second grade to solve.

Children can now learn to play dreidel in its traditional form. Dreidel can be a good activity for rainy or snowy days when outdoor recess is cancelled or as an activity in the room when other work has been completed.

A final thought for the second grade teacher. This year's winter festival preparations are a foundation for a later deepening of the Christian festivals. While the teacher should not neglect Chanukah altogether, she need not overemphasize it either. She can look at the school festivals and find ways in which the Jewish children's heritage may already be present. For instance, in preparing for Saint Nicholas Day, remember that the tangerines or dates for the children's shoes are two major crops in Israel. Even if the produce used is more national, the teacher can look at these gifts from Saint Nicholas as yet one more way in which the two traditions merge naturally without having to force them to do so.

Verses for Second Grade

EIGHT ARE THE LIGHTS
Eight are the lights
Of Chanuko.
We light for a week
And a day.
We kindle the lights,
And bless each other
And sing a song
And pray.

Eight are the lights
Of Chanuko
For justice and mercy
And love,
For charity, courage
And honor and peace,
And faith in Heaven
Above.
— Ilo Orleans[84]

NINE LITTLE CANDLES
Nine little candles—what a sight!
They stand in the menorah and look so bright.
This one said, "I want to sway."
This one said, "I'm melting away."
This one said, "I'm still pretty tall."
This one said, "I'm getting small."
This one said, "I feel like skipping."
This one said, "My wax is dripping."
This one said, "I have no more light."
This one said, "It's the last Chanukah night."
The shamash said with a shout,
"I'll be the last candle to go out!
For eight long days, we did burn.
We'll see you next Chanukah when we return."
— Sylvia Rouss[85]

Deborah, Woman of Flames[86]

by

Janet Zimmerman-Kahan

When Deborah was a young girl, she already knew that God intended her to do special things for her people. But she had no idea what they were to be. When she wasn't helping her mother, she went searching for her mission in life.

Of all places she went to look, the marketplace was best. The musty, sweet and tangy smells, the vendors trying to out-shout each other, the people pushing and shoving to find the best buys—all this thrilled her with the promise of unexpected happenings.

One day, in a far corner of the marketplace, in a dilapidated stall, she saw an old woman. Clad in drab rags, the woman sat on a stool with yards of hemp at her feet. She was making wicks for the lamps in the Holy Temple. As she moved her hands, the hemp seemed to leap and dance between her fingers, turning into strands of light. Deborah's heart leaped too, and she thought, "If only I could learn to make light as this woman does, I am sure my purpose in life would be fulfilled."

The old woman agreed to teach Deborah how to make wicks for the lamps in the Holy Temple. The work would be hard, Deborah was warned.

But Deborah persisted. At first the wicks she made barely cast any light at all. Instructing her, the old woman said, "You must allow the light inside your spirit to flow through your fingers and into the hemp itself."

"But how?" Deborah wanted to know.

"When you weave your wick, think of words of Torah, for they carry much light inside them," replied the old woman.

Deborah made ready to weave. She closed her eyes and thought of words which echoed the need of the time, a prayer for peace: *hiney ma tov u-mah nayim shevet achim gam yachad*.[87] She fixed her mind on these words until, like ripe pods, they burst forth with light. Pulsing within her and radiating out to her hands and fingers, the light grew in strength and brightness.

The wicks she made then were stronger than the previous ones. The strands appeared to vibrate as if they were the stems of the living plants from which they had sprung. When the old woman touched fire to the wick, the light burned brilliantly, filling the stall in which they sat.

Now that Deborah had mastered this step, she was ready to move on to the next. She was told, "This time as you weave your wick, open yourself to the light of God which is all around and has been since the Creation."

"But how?" Deborah wanted to know.

"Close your eyes and let your mind rest until it becomes as quiet as a pool of oil about to be sparked by God. Thoughts and worries will enter your mind and you will feel unequal to the task of bringing peace to your people. You will think of the factions within the tribes, of the strife which beleaguers the nation from within and from without. You will doubt your own abilities to do anything about this. But you will overcome these thoughts and rise above them."

Everything the old woman said came true. As soon as Deborah closed her eyes, she was plagued by thoughts of an insidious nature. She questioned how she would ever be able to conquer all those doubts and become a vessel for divine light.

She trained her mind on *hiney mah tov* again, this time considering the deeper meaning of the words. A calm and a strength flowed from them. She became one with the light permeating the words, until it seemed the entire marketplace and the world beyond were illuminated. As Deborah allowed her hands to do their familiar dance of hemp weaving, the light gathered strength, traveling throughout her entire body, unleashing the emotion and power she had stored within. Lights of gold and silver and pure white emanated from her and surrounded her as if she, herself, were a flame.

This time the wick was perfect, glowing before fire ever touched it. The old woman looked at Deborah and said, "You have learned all that I have to teach you. Now you will be called a Woman of Flames. You know the secret of making splendid lights for the Holy Temple. Let the light inside you illuminate all you do. Let the light bring your vision of peace into being."

Indeed Deborah's light continued to grow as she did. Deborah became a woman of importance, a prophetess, a woman of flames. She judged Israel in ancient days, bringing peace to her people and her land.

One Hanukkah in Helm[88]

by

Yaacov Luria

A beggar, a stranger, came to Helm, and the people shut their doors on him. It was the week of Hanukkah, a cold time. And yet the people of Helm, who were known everywhere for their kindness, peered through their frosted windowpanes at the ragged little man but kept their doors closed to his knocking.

How did such a thing happen? Helm, you see, was a very special place. An ordinary town had one or two, at most, a half dozen beggars. Helm was so poor that half the town had become beggars. This was a fine arrangement since no decent householder in Helm ever refused anyone asking for charity. One half of the townspeople gave alms. A rich man never worried that giving charity might make him poor. He could always turn beggar and get back the wealth he had given away.

To be sure, some people seem to be born to worry. One such worrier was Yoneh Shmeryl, the president of the Beggars' Benevolent Brotherhood of Helm. Yoneh Shmeryl's head, let me tell you, was like a clock: a hundred little wheels were turning inside it all the time.

Now, one day, as Yoneh Shmeryl was mending the thatch on the roof of his house, he fell to asking himself questions. All kinds of foolish questions came jumping at him like rabbits, but he had wise answers for all of them. Yet one question chilled him to his very bones: What would happen if, God forbid, there should be more beggars in Helm than there were charity-givers?

It took much stroking of his beard before he brought forth the answer: Some unfortunate chap would be without a patron. Without a patron there would be no charity. Without charity the poor man would starve—*oy gevalt*! A dreadful danger hung over the town! At once he called a meeting of the Beggars' Brotherhood in the synagogue. His fiery words of warning brought cold shudders to his fellow beggars. With one voice they cried out:

No strange beggars must henceforth be allowed in Helm. All doors must stay shut when they come knocking, not a penny should be given them. Otherwise the beggars pledged that they would leave in a body and take their business elsewhere.

What choice did the rest of the Helmites have? Without beggars Helm would be ruined! Everyone agreed: Let whatever the beggars demanded be done.

And so it was that the little man, a beggar from who knew where, came to Helm and found himself shunned. From the synagogue, of course, he could not be shut out. He sat warming himself by the stove, stuffing scraps of felt into the holes in his boots and thinking aloud to Gimpel Shammash.

"If only I had a crust of bread...," mused the beggar. "With a bread crust I could make latkes in honor of Hanukkah."

Gimpel straightened up so suddenly that his *yarmulkeh* almost fell off his head. "Latkes for Hanukkah from a crust of bread!" he cried. "Unbelievable!"

The stranger's sharp black eyes twinkled pleasantly. "Hanukkah is a holiday of miracles. I can do what I say."

All at once Gimpel felt the bravery within him. "I don't care what Yoneh Shmeryl will do," he told the stranger. "I will get you your bread." And he pulled his cloak tightly around him and rushed out into the cold.

"Don't forget a grater and a skillet. And maybe a mixing bowl!" the stranger called after him.

In less time than it takes to say the Eighteen Blessings, the *Shemoneh Esreh*, Gimpel had run to the baker and gotten a stale challah. From this one and that one he borrowed a skillet, a mixing bowl, a wooden ladle, and a grater. Whipped on by Gimpel, the secret came galloping through the town. "Hanukkah latkes from a crust of bread—imagine!" Everyone dropped what he was doing and followed Gimpel. At the head of the crowd marched Yoneh Shmeryl waving his rolled-up umbrella like a sword.

When they reached the synagogue, the stranger gave one and all a hearty *shalom aleikhem*, hitched up the sleeves of his robe, and began to grate the bread into the mixing bowl. When there was just a tiny heel of challah left, he stopped. "If I only had a few pinches of salt and pepper . . . ," he murmured.

In an instant someone brought forth salt and pepper shakers. Then the beggar sighed gently, "A drop of fat would be good too." Immediately a jug of goose fat appeared. Slowly, a very little at a time, he dusted the pepper and salt over the bread and poured the fat into the skillet.

Furiously Yoneh Shmeryl cried out, "Brother Jews, you are being fooled. From bread, salt, pepper, and goose fat you cannot make latkes!"

Said the stranger, "You may give me forty lashes if I lie." Yet his forehead furrowed in a frown, as if he were not quite satisfied.

Timidly, Gimpel reached into his pocket and produced an onion. The stranger's eyes lit up. "What harm can an onion do?" he asked.

Beyleh, the water carrier's widow, now spoke up. "I happen to have a few eggs in my shawl. Perhaps. . . ."

"Eggs? Why not eggs?" the stranger agreed, and into the bowl they went. And now he rubbed his hands together. "Ah, will you taste latkes now! Truthfully, there are some who insist that a touch of potatoes brings out the flavor just right. I like a simple batter."

At this point Shprintze the midwife, a woman as big as an elephant, held out two tremendous handfuls of potatoes. "Let it be a first-class miracle. Something to tell our great-grandchildren!" she trumpeted.

"With potatoes I can make latkes too," sneered Yoneh Shmeryl.

"You are right," agreed the stranger. "I don't need them."

"What—you refuse my gift?" cried Shprintze in such a terrible voice that the lamps in the synagogue flickered.

"No charity to strange beggars—you agreed!" bleated Yoneh Shmeryl. "Otherwise we leave Helm!"

"So leave! Go with my blessing!" bellowed Shprintze. She towered over the little stranger while he grated the potatoes and stirred them into the batter.

And suddenly a delicious aroma—warm and peppery and fatty good—came billowing through the synagogue—and there were latkes turning golden brown! The bellies of the Helmites rumbled. Hungrily they watched the little stranger scoop a pancake from the skillet, make a quick blessing, and begin crunching away.

Yoneh Shmeryl demanded, "I must taste for myself!" He devoured two pancakes and was biting into a third before he announced, "Helmites, these are the best potato pancakes I have ever eaten!"

"A miracle! A Hanukkah miracle!" cried the Helmites, and they came surging forward to taste the wonderful latkes.

And magically, more of everything sprang up—more skillets, more goose fat, more onions, more potatoes. As fast as the latkes were done, the Helmites gobbled them up. All at once they were singing and dancing. When everyone had danced and sung himself out, Yoneh Shmeryl himself carried the stranger off to spend the night on a warm feather bed.

Nu, it was almost Passover before the Helmites let the little miracle-maker go. They went back to their old ways, welcoming wayfarers with warm hearts and open hands. And their Hanukkahs after that were especially joyous, for they were remembering more than one miracle.

Now, Helmites, as you may have heard, were not the cleverest people in the world. Yet sometimes a wise child did arise among them. "Ah, what a head he has!" they would marvel. "Someday he will make latkes from bread crumbs yet!"

Chanukah in the Third Grade

The third grade winter season can be a time to focus more upon Chanukah. Although Chanukah is not part of the Old Testament, the third grade children develop a relationship with the Hebrew people of old. They have a sense of how these people experienced the world, each other, and their God. Third grade is the first time that the story of Chanukah as a military victory can be brought into the classroom, for the children now have a sense of the importance of the Jewish traditions and can imagine why the Maccabees would fight to preserve their heritage.

The third grader still lives in pictures and does not need an intellectual rendering of the Chanukah story. The poem "It Happened on Hanukkah" is a playful approach to this festival's story. The meter is similar to "'Twas the Night before Christmas," which is familiar to most children, making the reading of this long poem less daunting. The class could break up into reading groups and practice the poem, the stronger readers having larger sections and the struggling readers one or two stanzas. The class could then come back together and take turns reading, and possibly acting out, the verses. Another possible approach to this poem would be to read the first four stanzas the first day, then the first eight the second day and so on, until the whole poem is completed on the eighth day, which approach mimics the way in which the menorah is lit.

The story "Zlateh the Goat" by Isaac Bashevis Singer is a favorite Chanukah tale. While unfortunately not included here, it is one of his most popular stories and is easily found in libraries and bookstores. The collection of short stories also titled *Zlateh the Goat* has worked well as a reader for third grade students. The third grade curriculum of farming and practical work is particularly mirrored in this story. In it we see the difference between a child's relationship to the animal world and an adult relationship. Though the third grader may understand that the animal serves a purpose by providing milk and meat or by plowing, he still may have a hard time removing himself from the affections and attachments he has developed for the animal kingdom. This ability to look more objectively at animals occurs in the Human and Animal block in fourth grade. The story can also be seen as a reflection of the story of Isaac. Aaron is like Abraham, offering up a beloved one because that is what his father has demanded for the welfare of the family, and Zlateh is like Isaac, trusting of Aaron and offering unconditional love, regardless of her own fate. While this story need not be discussed in these terms with the third grade, the teacher may enjoy pondering the similarities as a way to bring the Old Testament into Chanukah.

If the third grade did not hear the story of Deborah last year, it would be a very fitting story for this year. In fact, if the class has been singing "H'nei Mah Tov" without knowing the story of Deborah, it would be appropriate to tell the story at this time.

Since the third grade year focuses on the Hebrew people, the teacher can bring some Chanukah songs in Hebrew to the class. A fun Hebrew song the children can learn is "S'vivon." Since the class may already be familiar with "Oh Hanuka" or "Hanukah" in English, it might be fun to switch to the Hebrew version. The teacher can write the transliteration on the board or have the children come to the board and write out what it sounds like to them. This would remind the children that there are various ways of expressing through writing the sounds that we hear and can serve as a review, especially of diphthongs. Because transliteration is not meant to look like the written word, only to sound like it, there is no right or wrong. This might be especially helpful for the children who are struggling with spelling and also have low self-esteem.

The game "Eight" is a fun math review activity the third grade might enjoy. The rules are as follows:

> Players are seated in a circle. The first player starts to count, saying: "one," and each player continues the count. Whenever the count is eight, a multiple of eight (16, 24, 32, etc.), or includes eight (18, 28, 38, etc.), the

player whose turn it is does not count but stands up and says, "Chanukah." A player who errs or misses is eliminated from the game.[89]

This game could also be played by breaking up into smaller groups, so that the play could be faster and there would be less opportunity to plan ahead.

In keeping with the third grade cooking theme, the class can make latkes. The third grade teacher can find out if the second grade will be hearing the story "One Hanukkah in Helm." If so, the third grade can plan to surprise the second grade by providing latkes for them at the end of the story or on the following day. If the third grade made applesauce in the fall, now is the time to bring it out and share it with any other latke parties in the school.

The third grade year emphasizes the traditional arts. Menorah making is a traditional craft of the Hebrew people. The teacher might ask families to share their menorahs and any stories of their heritage. It is ideal if the class can see menorahs made from a variety of materials. There are nearly as many types of menorahs as there are Jews to kindle them! After looking at menorahs of clay, glass, stone, wood, dough, and so forth, the third graders could design their own menorahs. The teacher may have the class draw their designs, or she may wish to provide materials for them to make simple individual menorahs. Most Jewish holiday books for children provide examples and instructions for making menorahs. A Waldorf teacher could be quite creative with the resources available in the school.

There can be a lot of outer activity involved in the third grade's experience of Chanukah. Yet it should be remembered that the third grader, poised on the precipice of illumination that is the nine-year change, is, in fact, living the metaphor of Chanukah. It is the task of the teacher to bring the children through their darker days by kindling their individual flames.

Verses for Third Grade

U<small>NTITLED</small>
>We are the candle
>lit by a spark from God.
>Toward the heavens
>our bright flame reaches,
>adding light to the world around us.
>So fragile this flame . . . .
>>– "Vataher Libenu," Congregation Beth El
>>of the Sudbury River Valley[90]

I<small>T</small> H<small>APPENED ON</small> H<small>ANUKKAH</small>
>It happened on Hanukkah, so it is said,
>When all of the children had gone up to bed,
>The classroom was empty, and everything still,
>The first candle flickered alone on the sill.
>
>Silence and darkness and no one around,
>Just household utensils alone on the ground.
>They trembled together, a little from cold.
>And a little from fear, so the story is told.
>
>And each one was thinking: "What's that? Did you hear?
>The wind whispered something, just now, in my ear.
>Why does the floor seem to crackle and spark?
>And what's crawling toward me from out of the dark?
>
>"Who whistled? It wasn't a cricket, I know.
>The sound was so strange, and it frightened me so.
>A terrible something will happen tonight. . . .
>You'll see before sunrise, I'm perfectly right."
>
>The table was shaking—it really was scared.
>The chair would have yelled out for help if it dared.
>An old, worn-out broom standing up at the wall
>Was even afraid to be frightened at all.
>The puppy among them, too small yet to growl,
>Almost fainted each time that he heard the wind howl.

It ended when suddenly, out of the gloom,
In a voice made of iron and sounding like doom,
The clock on the shelf gathered courage and spoke,
"What's going on? Is this some kind of joke?

"This one is trembling and that one is tense.
The third one is moody—it doesn't make sense.
What are you anyway? Honored utensils
Or tatters and dishrags and old pointless pencils?"

The utensils awoke, as it seemed, from a dream
And with one voice, together they let out a scream,
"Shut up, stupid ticker, up there on the shelf.
You're only a dirty old dishrag yourself.

"Look here! Pay attention! No cowards are we.
We haven't forgotten what fun 'fun' can be.
Come on, let's get started. We'll set up a game
Just to put that old tick-tocking timepiece to shame."

When all the utensils were quiet at last
The broom in the corner gave out with a blast,
"The Hanukkah game—we know every rule.
Let's play it and shut up that tick-tocking fool.

"Let's start with me, with my beard I'll admit it,
It's made out of straw, but it's really exquisite.
So with your permission, without any bother,
I'll be Mattathias, the Maccabees' father.

"And you, little potbellied stove over there,
You will be Judah, my son and my heir.
So get up—there's a war and you've got to take part
With the hot burning flame of the Lord for your heart.

"What we need now are some brothers for you,
And for these parts, I think that the cacti will do.
Into battle we're going, you brave fighting flowers.
Your spikes must be sharpened for hours and hours."

The broom kept on giving out parts to his men
'Til he came to the Syrian Soldiers. And then
He grew quiet. Nobody grabbed for the part
And each of them wanted to cry in his heart.
For they knew very well, and it wasn't a mystery,
Syria lost in the pages of history.

The chairs got together and quickly decided
And then, to the rest, their decision confided,
"We'll be the Syrians, worry no more.
We're twice the men you are, our legs number four.
Shall we be afraid of the Maccabees' force?
We'll beat them on foot and we'll beat them on horse."

The teapots came marching in militial rows,
And each one was waving his long crooked nose.
The chairs gaily thundered, "Our elephants, they—
We'll murder the Maccabees. . . . Hip, hip, hooray.
From this time forward, we all can be sure
That under our king we'll be safe and secure."

"Our king," cried a chair. "Who's the king?" No one spoke,
For no one was willing to carry the yoke.
They all shook their heads and gave out with a sigh,
"I'm not Antiochus the Madman, not I."

The game was in danger of falling apart,
For, lacking a ruler, the play had no heart.
An elephant wandered around like a mourner
Until he bumped into the pup in the corner,
When lifting him up in the air with his nose
He trumpeted, "Here he is. Anything goes."

The poor little puppy, he cried and whined,
He squirmed and he twisted—went out of his mind,
He scratched and he bit, oh, how bravely he fought.
But nothing could help him; the puppy was caught.

When they saw his reluctance, the elephant said,
"Hush up and be king. You're our chief and our head.
If you try to escape—and you'd better not dare—
If you do, you'll be captured and tied to a chair."

With everything ready the game could begin
And Judah yelled loudly, his face in a grin,
"Take care, Antiochus, watch out what you're doing.
My anger is boiling and cooking and stewing.

"My city, Jerusalem, leave it alone,
Or I'll beat you so hard that I'll break every bone.
When I've finished, your moldy old corpse I'll bequeath
To the birds of the sky and the beasts underneath."

The puppy cried out to his mother in fright,
"Mommy, why does this potbellied stove want to fight?
I'm not the king of the Syrian host.
I'm just a poor puppy who'll soon be a ghost."

The little pup's cries didn't help anymore,
For suddenly—whack—the beginning of war,
And before he could find a dark corner to hide in,
A big chair fell over and half crushed his side in.

The sounds of the battle rose up from the floor
From cellar to rafters and on out the door:
The shouts of the brave and cries of the weak,
The laugh of the mighty, the moans of the meek.

The brave Judah Maccabee lowered his sword,
And swung it with joy at the Syrian horde.
His flying locks burned as the sword rose and fell,
And he looked like a devil come straight out of hell.

The broom, Mattathias, yelled out from the side,
"You're a warrior, Son, full of courage and pride.
Let's go forward, you Maccabees, let your swords ring
'Til we capture the Madman, the Syrian king.

"That's the way, that's the way—forward we go."
Then in charged the elephants, straight in a row.
"Come on, wake up, boys, we're really in trouble.
The elephants must be turned back—on the double.

And chaos arose, and a dreadful confusion.
It looked like a terrible nightmare illusion.
Head against head and chest against chest,
And hand against hand, without any rest.

The dreidel alone, being calm and serene,
Whirled forward and backward, surveying the scene.
Being brilliant and clever, he's making a test,
To discover which army will come out the best.

For, being quite clever, and being quite wise,
And wanting to know who would take home the prize,
"I'll wait till the end of the battle," he thought,
"And I'll know how to choose once the battle's been fought."

But wait just a moment! The Syrian men
Are retreating. . . . The Maccabees conquer again.
And Judah cries, "Yippee! Hurrah! Look and see,
We've won freedom and light with our great victory."

The dreidel stopped spinning and fell on his side.
He stretched out on the floor and he happily cried,
"Victory, victory, do you all hear?
A wonderful miracle happened right here."

— Nathan Alterman
Translated by Steve Friedman[91]

Chanukah in the Fourth Grade

The fourth graders are by now quite familiar with the rituals of Chanukah. For three years they have cooked, played dreidel, lit candles, and sung folk songs. In class and in winter assemblies, they have heard many stories of Chanukah. Up to this point the military aspect of the holiday has been downplayed, but now both the warrior and trickster spirits of the Norse myths can be channeled into the Chanukah celebration.

In the poem "A Hanukkah Top," the terrain of the Maccabees is viewed through the lens of a dreidel. The emphasis of the poem is not on military victory but on the victory over the land itself. While reminiscent of farming in third grade, this poem reflects the focus on geography in fourth grade. The theme of local geography can be reinforced in an activity that comes from the book *My Very Own Chanukah*. Reflecting on the story of Chanukah, focus on how a small group of people could outwit a large army. One of the reasons the Maccabees did so well was because they were fighting in their own territory (on their own "turf"). The town of Modin was small and the villagers knew the subtleties of their geographical surroundings. The Maccabees were able to outwit the Syrians by popping up in unexpected places and surprising their enemy. The fourth grade teacher could tell the story from the point of view of a Maccabee: Describe where the secret hiding places were, what they looked like, how the knowledge of their immediate surroundings helped them to protect their families. The next day the teacher can have the children make a map of their own neighborhood, focusing on the secret hiding places for people and objects or notes. Are there places that would be conducive to laying a trap? How would it look on the map? The teacher could also use this as a composition topic. If the children were Maccabees how would the story about the battle against the Syrians unfold in their own neighborhood?[92]

The focus of the above activities is not on the warrior element, but rather the trickster element. This mirrors the characteristics of Loki in the Norse myths. The story "How to Sell a Menorah" further emphasizes the trickster qualities of the fourth grade year. In "How to Sell a Menorah," the trickery is quite willful. The desire to take advantage of others for one's own benefit is related unabashedly. This story speaks to the nine- or ten-year-old who may be in a stage of testing social boundaries. If the teacher wishes to contrast this story with a story of a girl whose trickery benefits others rather than harming them, I recommend the story "Hannah the Joyful," which can be found in Nina Jaffe's book, *The Uninvited Guest*.

The fourth grade may also enjoy a Chanukah mind teaser. The teacher writes the name "Judah Maccabee" on the board and the children try to make as many words out of the letters in a given number of minutes (five to ten). The words are scored as follows: 3 letters = 1 point, 4 letters = 2 points, 5 letters = 4 points, 6 letters = 5 points, 7 letters = 10 points.[93]

If the fourth grade has embarked on math word problems, then they might try this tricky Chanukah problem:

> Three brothers bought three menorahs for a total of $60. After the brothers left the store, the shopkeeper realized he had made a mistake. The menorahs should have been sold for $55. He gave the clerk five $1 bills and told him to run after the brothers. Each brother took $1 from the clerk. The brothers thanked him, wished him a happy Chanukah and told him to keep the extra $2. With the $1 the clerk returned to each of them, the brothers had paid a total of $57 for the menorahs. Add to the $57 the $2 the clerk kept and you have just $59. What happened to the other dollar?
>
> *The shopkeeper has $55 and the brothers have $3. That makes $58. Add to that the $2 the brothers gave the clerk and you have $60.*[94]

A great way to channel the fourth graders' natural inclination to play with words and push the boundaries a bit is to let them write their own silly verses to the dreidel song. I found my students to be extremely adept at creating their own charming verses. In fact, we heard new verses every day for three weeks! Some of the children's verses are:

> I had a little dreidel
> I made it out of chalk,
> And when I tried to spin it,
> It drew on the sidewalk.

and

> I made it out of paint . . .
> I felt like I would faint.

and

> I made it out of snow . . .
> I watched a puddle grow!

This became one of our contributions to the winter assembly and is still remembered years later by the community.

There are a few Chanukah rounds that the fourth grade can learn to sing, such as "Once an Evil King" and the traditional "Who Can Retell?" "Shalom Chavarim" is not a traditional Chanukah song but its message of peace fits the holiday theme. Since many of the Norse stories and some of the suggested Chanukah activities are accounts of warriors and tricksters, it is balancing to enliven the children with the lyrics "sing peace and goodwill." This also helps make a connection to the messages of Advent and Christmas.

Verses for Fourth Grade

A Hanukkah Top

Turn my top, around, around,
Past the bush and pit and mound,
Past the vineyards, brook, and rill,
Past the valley and the hill,
On to Kishon, as you veer,
When you meet a pioneer,
Tell your legend, bring him cheer:
"Miracles have happened here!"

Once this land was swampy, friend,
Now to that has come an end.
Conquered where the waste and mud
In a battle void of blood;
Not with swords was won the soil,
But with ceaseless, endless toil.

Unto Modin swiftly fly,
And your tidings shout and cry:
"Maccabeans, rest in peace,
Lo, your valiant heirs increase.
In the vanguard they wage war,
Planting vineyards by the score,
Swinging hammers, hauling loads,
Building houses, paving roads. . . ."

Tell your legend, bring him cheer:
"Miracles are happening here!"

– Nahum D. Karpivner
Translated by Harry H. Fein[95]

I LIKE LATKES

    I like latkes
    They taste fine.
    I'll put potatoes
    and oil in mine.
    I'll put in butter
    and lots of salt,
    strawberry jam
    and chocolate malt.
    Vinegar, bubble gum,
    peanuts and paste,
    carrot juice, jelly
    and lemon to taste.
    I like latkes.
    They taste fine.
    But I'd never, ever
    eat one of mine.

                – David A. Adler[96]

How to Sell a Menorah![97]

by

Peninnah Schram

Hershele Ostropolier the prankster was always looking for new ways to make a few kopeks. Not that he had any intention of working for a living—Heaven forbid! Rather, he earned by his wits and his tongue. After all, he had been appointed jester to Rabbi Boruch of Miedziboz and he had to keep finding new ways and words to lift the rabbi out of his melancholia. But he also had to invent ways to match wits with the rabbi in order to get his wages. More often than not, as a matter of fact, he did not get paid. Then Hershele would say to himself, "My name isn't Hershele for nothing. Take advantage of me, and you'll pay dearly for it." What would Hershele do? Doing what he did best, he would tell the rabbi a good story, a story with such convoluted logic, yet with such a clear lesson, that in the end, the rabbi would be shamed into paying Hershele his wages.

Always a pauper, always fighting poverty, Hershele was also hungry. Once he went into an inn for a meal. Seeing this disheveled, scary looking fellow, the innkeeper's wife, who was alone in the inn, became frightened and refused to serve him. "We have no more food left in the kitchen," she said.

"Well, then I'll have to do what my father always did," announced Hershele in a loud voice.

Becoming even more alarmed about what he might do, the innkeeper's wife ran to the kitchen and brought out a veritable feast. Hershele ate with a hearty appetite. Then, as she watched Hershele drinking his glass of tea, the innkeeper's wife, feeling calmer, approached him and asked in a timid voice, "So what would your father always do?"

With a big grin, Hershele replied, "When my father had no food, he went hungry."

Now Hershele was hardly a lazy man, for it was more than a full-time job for him to avenge all the insults he received, wheedle money (even from his wife!), outsmart unsuspecting innkeepers for a meal, and especially when he was slighted or rebuffed, even teach a greedy man or rogue a lesson. "Just you wait, you rogue! My name isn't Hershele for nothing! Insult me to your heart's content. You'll pay dearly for it."

Hershele never used violence to achieve his goals. His weapon was words, and the arrow always reached its mark. Not only did the person learn the lesson, but Hershele gained a meal or a few kopeks at the same time. The saying "He who laughs last, laughs best" could have been invented just for Hershele.

Hershele was thinking very hard about his next few kopeks, particularly where they would come from. "Holidays are especially good times for earning a few kopeks," he thought. "And there are certainly plenty of holidays. Soon it will be Chanukah. Chanukah, of course! What does every Jew need for Chanukah? A menorah!"

So Hershele set out to find a tinsmith who would make a bagful of menorahs for him, all of the same size and design. Finally he found one who—unbelievably—agreed to his terms. The tinsmith would give Hershele the menorahs on consignment; after Hershele got paid, the tinsmith would get paid.

During the last few days before Chanukah, Hershele went around town selling his menorahs. On the morning before Chanukah, with only a few menorahs left, Hershele entered the shop of a wealthy shopkeeper who was as stingy as he was rude. Hershele pulled a menorah from his bag and placed it on the table. "It's time to buy the menorah," he said. "And this is the finest one I have, especially suited for such a prominent citizen as yourself. I have saved this one just for you."

The wealthy shopkeeper barely glanced up from his books and replied, "No, no, I'm not interested. I have a menorah from last year that will do just fine. My wife will find it and prepare it for lighting."

But Hershele was not to be put off by a simple no. "Do you like latkes?" he asked.

"I love latkes," replied the shopkeeper, patting his large stomach.

"Well, then, can you imagine your wife searching all afternoon for the menorah and discovering, when she finally finds it, that one of the candle holders has broken off? Then what would she do? I'll tell you what she would do. She would have to search through the town for another menorah, and who knows if she could find one just before the holiday? By then, it would be almost dark. And then she wouldn't have time to peel all the potatoes and grate them and make the beautiful potato latkes you love so much. And what kind of *yom tov* would it be without lighting the candles and with no latkes? Think how sorry you would be that you didn't buy this menorah from me."

By now, all the shopkeeper wanted was to be rid of Hershele, so he bought the menorah.

Hershele quickly left the shop and rushed to the shopkeeper's house. When the shopkeeper's wife came to the door, Hershele was standing there with a menorah in his hand. "I just came from your husband's shop and he asked me to tell you not to look for last year's menorah. He said you should just buy a new one from me." Hershele held the menorah out to the shopkeeper's wife and, well, what could she do? She bought the menorah from Hershele.

That evening, the wealthy man arrived home with the menorah he had bought from Hershele safely bundled in layers of paper. When he had unwrapped it, he carried it into the living room for his wife to see. And there she stood, holding a menorah exactly like the one he carried.

"Where did you get that menorah?" questioned the husband.

"From Hershele, of course. Just as you told me to," answered the wife.

"I told you? Who told you?" the husband shouted.

"Hershele! Hershele has tricked us both into buying from him!"

The wealthy man motioned angrily to his servant and said, "Find Hershele and bring him to me."

The servant went to Hershele's house, and finding him there, he said, "My master wants to see you immediately. Come quickly, before it's time to light the Chanukah menorah."

"Oh, your master must want to buy a menorah from me," said Hershele. "My menorahs are the best there are. But why did he wait until the last minute to buy one? By the time I go to his house and sell him a menorah and return home, it will be past the time to light the candles. So I'll tell you what. Why don't you just give me the money and I'll give you the menorah and you can take it to your master."

That's what happened. And that's how to sell a menorah!

Chanukah wicks total 9
The candles to light are 8
The days of the week are 7
The latkes to eat are 6
The pennies to give are 5
The sides of a dreidel are 4
Menorahs the miser bought are 3
The blessings over the candles are 2
And Hershele, master trickster, is 1
And now the tale is done!

Chanukah in the Fifth Grade

The fifth grade curriculum brings the children to the times preceding the story of Chanukah. As the fifth grade journeys through the epochs, they should experience them first with awe and only later with a more discriminating eye. These epochs, times of struggle, resistance and slavery, were difficult for the Jewish people. The teacher may or may not choose to address this with her class.

The study of Ancient Greece will come after wintertime, so delving into the traditional story of Chanukah is still slightly premature. But the children will most likely have learned about ancient Persia by the time Chanukah arrives. If they have "slept on" the block, they can now remember it through someone else's story.

In the fifth grade study of ancient cultures we begin to separate myth, history and biography. The story of Judith has become a traditional part of the Chanukah liturgy and is fitting for this age. Although it pre-dates the Chanukah story, taking place in the Assyrian age, this tale of courage and resistance resembles the story of the Maccabees. The story of Judith takes us a step back from the military victory of Chanukah and addresses what one person can do with cunning rather than might. In this story a woman stands up for her beliefs even when discouraged by those around her. She shows no fear, but she is also a woman with nothing to lose. Judith is a widow, alone in the world, willing to take risks. Judith is a woman of action while others would rather concede and complain about their lot in life. As fifth graders are approaching pre-adolescence, this story may stir something in them.

There are two versions of the Judith story included in the fifth grade Chanukah curriculum. The teacher may prefer the prose version if there is not a lot of time available. The version in verse is longer and could be used as a reader. Like the Greek epics, this poem also lends itself to recitation, either individual or choral. The teacher is encouraged to read through the whole poem as a source for speech work during the eight days of Chanukah, even if the entirety of the poem is too much for the class.

The story of Judith has inspired the Chanukah tradition of eating cheese. The fifth grade can plan a cheese party as part of a snack or lunch. Each child can bring cubes of a favorite cheese for others to sample (tofu-cheese can be substituted for the dairy-free children). The children could then see how much cheese it takes before they need to drink!

There is another Chanukah tradition based on the Judith story, which is one of the only preserved stories in which a woman saves the Jewish people. Because of this, women are especially honored during Chanukah. The tradition is that on the seventh day of Chanukah the women light the candles and do no more work. The implication is that on the other seven days, the women still do all the work of the house once the menorah lights have extinguished. The seventh day is different. If it falls on a school day, the fifth grade teacher could have the seventh day of Chanukah be a day of rest for the girls in the class. The fifth grade history curriculum tends to be male-dominated, so this may be a nice way to turn the tables for a day. The boys could clean up for the girls after snack and lunch and do other classroom jobs for them. This might also be a way to bridge the growing gender gap often seen in the middle school as hormones begin to change the relationships within a class.

The music for Chanukah in the fifth grade also can reflect the story of Judith. "Not by Might" is a very popular Chanukah song that is full of vigor. Although it speaks more to nonviolence, Judith's determination can also be the "spirit." If the class did not learn "Who Can Retell?" last year as a round, they can learn it this year. Whether learning it anew or bringing it back for a second year, this additional verse can be used:

> Who can retell the things which befell us?
> Who can count them?
> In every age, the women are sage,

And show their strength.
Hear! At this time of year in days of yore,
The moon did wane, and then her light restore,
And today our people in rebirth,
Will unite, arise, and heal the earth.[98]

As in fourth grade, the poem "My Dreidel," uses the top as a symbol to cover distances. In this poem the dreidel goes to the lands of the history curriculum. Yet the tone of the poem reflects the study of geography. The fifth grader still enjoys playing games and the dreidel need not be dropped as an activity. In the beginning of this poem it seems like the dreidel is "growing up," but the end of the poem is full of child-like delight. Perhaps this poem can also serve as a reflection of the fifth grade child. At times he seems ready to venture out into the adult world, while at other times he wants to crawl into the teacher's lap and be a first grader once again.

Verse for Fifth Grade

MY DREIDEL
Come, my dreidel, my dreidel of tin,
Dance about merrily, dance and spin!
  Go swift, go far,
  And shining bright,
  Find the star
  Of my delight.

Spin to India, Afric-land,
Spin away over desert sand.
  No toil or lack
  Will spoil my pleasure,
  When you come back
  Bringing treasure.

Come, my dreidel, merrily scale
The towering hill, and span the vale.
> Over the prairie
> Dance and reel,
> Light and airy,
> Like a spinning wheel.

Make way for my dreidel, his whirl and sweep,
One step is a league, and a mile his leap.
> He's off with a bound
> Like a stallion bold.
> Hurrah! He has found
> A mountain of gold!

Rush to the mountain! Make way, make way!
Seize the treasure without delay!
> Win it, O
> My dreidel of tin,
> Before my foe
> Can say, 'I win!'

The dreidel swayed and shuddered once,
And then went backwards—oh, oh, you dunce!
> It wavered, strained,
> No longer bold.
> It had not gained
> The mountain of gold.

Tipsy, it staggered, backed, until
Down it went—my heart stood still...
> Gimel! Oh, joy!
> Come all and see
> How my spinning toy
> Has won for me.

– Hayyim Nahman Bialik
Translated by Deborah Pessin[99]

THE STORY OF JUDITH[100]

(Paraphrased from The Jerusalem Bible, *this story was contemporary to Maccabean times and was probably written about 100 B.C.E. It was preserved by the Catholic Church as Apocrypha.)*

It was the eighteenth year (587 B.C.E.) of the reign of Nebuchadnezzar, who ruled over the Assyrians in the great city of Nineveh (the place to which Jonah went). He sent for Holofernes, general-in-chief of his armies and said, "Be on your way. Take men of proved valor and advance against the western lands. The feet of my soldiers will cover the whole face of the earth and I will plunder it. Their wounded will fill the valleys, and the torrents and the rivers, blocked with their dead, will overflow. I will lead them captive to the ends of the earth. Now go!"

So Holofernes went with his whole army. He razed all the fortified towns, butchering all who offered him resistance. He burned the tents of the nomads and plundered their sheep runs. He set fire to fields, destroyed flocks and herds, sacked the towns, laid the countryside waste, and put all the young men to the sword. Holofernes even demolished the shrines and sacred trees of the people who surrendered, carrying out his commission to destroy all local gods and to force the nations to worship Nebuchadnezzar alone and to compel men of every language and nationality to hail him as a god. Fear and trembling seized all the coastal peoples.

When the Israelites living in Judea heard how Holofernes had treated the various nations, they were thoroughly alarmed at his approach and trembled for Jerusalem and the Temple. Their return from captivity (in Persia) had been only a short time before, as was the resettlement of the people and the reconsecration of the Temple. Joakim, the high priest, instructed the inhabitants of Bethulia and Betommesthaim to send men to occupy the mountain passes, which were the only access to Judea, to halt the attacking force. Then all the people of Israel prayed and cried most fervently to God. The people and the priests fasted, wore sackcloths and ashes, and made offerings.

Holofernes and his army laid siege to the town of Bethulia, capturing the spring that supplied water to the town. The Israelites of Bethulia eventually grew weak and collapsed from thirst. The people pleaded with the town elders to surrender. Uzziah, the mayor, convinced the people to wait five more days for God to act to bring help before they surrendered. Everyone went home from the town meeting despondent.

Judith, a wealthy and beautiful widow, lived in Bethulia. She was a God-fearing woman with a good reputation. She heard of the town meeting and the oath of Uzziah and was furious. She summoned the town elders and reprimanded them for testing God. Uzziah replied, "Everything you have said has been spoken from sincerity of heart and no one will contradict a word of it. From your earliest years all the people have known how shrewd you are and of how sound a heart. Now today is the first time your wisdom has been displayed. But the people are parched with thirst and we are forced to act. You are a devout woman. Pray to God for a downpour to fill our cistern."

Judith replied, "Listen to me. I intend to do something, the memory of which will be handed down to the children of our race from age to age. Tonight you must be at the gate of the town. I shall make my way out with my attendant. Before the time fixed by you for surrendering the town to our enemies, God will make use of me to rescue Israel. You must not ask what I intend to do; I will not tell you until I have done it."

Uzziah said, "Go in peace. May God show you a way to take revenge on our enemies."

Judith prayed mightily to God. Then she took off her widow's clothes. She bathed, anointed herself with perfumes, dressed her hair, and put on a dress she used to wear for joyful occasions when her husband had been alive. She put sandals on her feet and wore all her jewelry. Then she gave her attendant flasks of wine and oil, loaves of bread, and cakes of barley and dried fruit. All these provisions were wrapped for their journey. Judith and her attendant met Uzziah and the town elders at the town gates. They admired her beauty and how different she looked, and they prayed for her success. Then Judith and her maid left Bethulia.

They were immediately captured by the Assyrians. Judith told them she had vital information for Holofernes with which he would be able to conquer the town. She was brought to the tent of Holofernes, and Judith flattered him profusely. She then told him that the people of Bethulia, in their desperate circumstances, would sin against God. God would then deliver them into the hands of Holofernes and his armies. Judith said she was disgusted by the behavior of her neighbors and so had fled to Holofernes. She said, "I am a devout woman who honors God day and night. I propose to stay with you, my lord. I will go every night into the valley and pray to God to let me know when the people of Bethulia have committed their sin. I will then come and tell you, so that you can march out with your whole army and defeat them. All this has been foretold to me and I have been sent to reveal it to you." Holofernes and his men were very impressed with Judith and agreed to her plan.

Holofernes then had his banquet laid out for them to dine. But Judith would not eat the food, saying she must eat from her own provisions for fear of incurring God's wrath and ruining Holofernes's victory. Holofernes agreed and Judith ate her own food while he feasted. His servants then took Judith to a tent where she slept until midnight. She arose and sent a request to Holofernes that she and her maid be allowed to go out of the camp and pray. Holofernes ordered his guards not to prevent her. Judith stayed in the camp three days; each night she went out to pray and then returned to the camp and stayed in her tent until the evening meal.

On the fourth day, Holofernes gave a banquet for his personal staff. He invited Judith with the intent of seducing her. The general had ordered many delicacies and wines for their meal but Judith unpacked her own meal from a large bag. She politely insisted on eating only her own kosher food from her own dishes. They ate and drank for many hours, Holofernes drinking much more than he ever had in his life. It grew late, and the staff was dismissed. Judith told his chief of staff that she would again be going out to pray later and instructed her maid to wait outside close by. By this time, Holofernes had passed out drunk on his bed. Judith was alone in the tent with him. Judith took Holofernes's scimitar and with all her strength cut off his head. She tore down the bed canopy with the insignia. She gave the head of Holofernes and the canopy to her maid who put it in her food bag. The two women left the camp, climbed the slope to Bethulia and entered the town.

All the people of Bethulia rushed to greet Judith and her maid. As they all gathered around, Judith pulled the canopy out of the bag to show everyone the head of Holofernes. All the people cheered, worshipped God, and blessed Judith.

At daybreak, the head of Holofernes was hung on the ramparts of Bethulia. The Assyrian army was gripped with panic and fled Judea in retreat. Joakim, the high priest, came to Bethulia from Jerusalem to congratulate Judith. Judith led them in hymn to God, and everyone danced back to Jerusalem to make offerings to God at the Temple.

Judith's fame grew and grew over the years. Before she died she emancipated her maid. Judith lived to be one hundred five years old and all of Israel mourned her death for seven days.

Who Can Despise a People with Women Like This?
(The Book of Judith)[101]

Then Judith kneeled,
put her face in the dust,
stripped to the sackcloth she wore underneath—
just at the moment the evening incense offering
wafted to the Temple ceiling in Jerusalem—
cupped her face in her hands
and spoke,
her words rising outspoken
from her heart to the open sky—
an offering, a prayer:

"Lord, God of my fathers,
of Simon in whose hand You put a sword
to reward the strangers,
Lord, crush their violence,
break their thoughts to bits in Your anger
at their shameless threats of power.

"They want to force their way into Your sanctuary,
to cut off the ancient horn on your altar,
to strip bare the ark
in which You are held whole,
to demean Your spirit with swords of tin and iron,
to debase Your name.

"Look at the arrogance of their thoughts.
Cut them off in outrage,
bow their heads in shame,
sweep a mental sword through their minds.

"Put your sword in the hand of a widow.
Give me the presence of mind
to overpower them with pointed speech
in the sheath of an alluring voice,
to confuse them with an inner truth,
shaping words of steel
to slay 'equally' masters with their slaves,

servant and petty lord,
while they are inflated by selfish desire,
while they are charmed by feminine lips,
while they are caught in their self-deception.
Shatter their pride,
disperse their power
by a woman's hand.

"Your force is not visible in numbers, and armor
does not stand at attention before men of war.
Your power is indivisible and disarms violence,
and You are a Lord to the powerless,
help to the oppressed,
support to the weak, refuge to the humble,
a sudden rescue, a savior to the lost,
warmth in the coldest despair,
light in the most hopeless eyes.

"Please hear me, God of my father,
Lord of Israel's heritage,
Master of the universe, Creator of earth and sky,
King of all creation.
Hear my psalm.

"Let my words be lies they cannot hear.
Sharpen my tongue with charm,
my lips irresistible,
mirroring their inner deceit
which stares back into their surprised faces,
as my words cut deep
like a sudden knife
into those with cruel plans
against our heart, against Your spirit,
and the Temple of Your spirit."

Judith's prayer was over.
She rose from the ground,
called to her maid,
and in the house removed the sackcloth
and widow's dress, then bathed
in creams and expensive perfumes,

and did her hair
crowned with a subtle tiara,
and put on her most attractive dress,
not worn since her husband Manasseh died,
and before that only on joyous occasions—
slender sandals adorned her feet
brightened by jeweled anklets,
bracelets and rings on her arms and fingers,
earrings and pins and other jewelry,
making up such a beautiful picture
that any man or woman's head would turn.

She gave her maid flasks of oil and a skin of wine,
fig cakes and dried fruit,
a bag filled with barley cakes and roasted grains,
cheeses,
and loaves of sweetest challah,
then carefully wrapped her own dishes
and koshered pottery,
also for her maid to carry.

They kept walking straight across the valley
until sighted by Assyrian advance troops
who seized Judith, interrogated her,
"Where do you come from?
What people do you belong to?
Where are you going?"

"I'm a daughter of Hebrews
but I'm escaping from them
because they are fodder for you
to be devoured as simply as grain in a bowl.
I want to be taken to Holofernes, your Lord.
I can report the truth to him,
I want to show him the simplest way
to take over the mountains and approaches
surrounding this country
without losing a single man,
subduing it without so much as a bruise."

As these men listened to her well-chosen words,
they saw the noble beauty in Judith's face
and (coupled with her directness)
they were overwhelmed
by such physical elegance in a woman.
"You have saved your life
not hesitating to come directly
into the presence of our lord.
You will be taken straight to his tent
and we will announce you to him—
have no fear in your heart
when you are in his presence
because when you tell him what you told us
he will treat you with deep respect."
A detachment of a hundred men
escorted the two women.

So Judith and her maid came safely
to the tent of Holofernes—
but not without causing a stir in the whole camp.
The news was buzzing from tent to tent,
and while Judith waited outside the commander's tent,
a crowd gathered around her,
amazed at her beauty.
This was the first they'd seen of an Israelite
and, coupled with what they'd heard,
they were amazed at the presence of this people.
As their curiosity fed on her grace,
"Who can despise a people with women like this?"
they were saying.
"We'll have to wipe out this entire race,
every last one of them,
just as we were told to do
because any that survive will probably outwit
just about anyone in the world—
moved simply by the agony of loss
of such grace and beauty
to bring our world to its knees
as surely as a disarmed suitor."

Then Holofernes's personal guards came out
to escort Judith into the tent
where he was resting on his bed
under the fine gauze mosquito net
that was a precious, royal canopy,
purple interwoven with fine strands of gold,
studded with emeralds
and many other gems: as stunning as a crown.

When Judith was announced, he came out,
silver lamps carried by servants leading the way,
into the front part of the tent,
and he saw her standing there and was amazed
at so beautiful a face.
She bowed touching her face to the ground
in homage, but his servants quickly lifted her up.
"Feel at ease, woman,"
Holofernes was saying.
"Have no fear in your heart.
I've never hurt anyone who made the choice
to serve Nebuchadnezzar, king of this world.
I did not choose to raise a spear
against your people in the hills.
They've brought me here themselves,
insulting me by taking us lightly.
Now tell me why you've escaped from them
to join us—but first, be at ease.
You have saved your life,
take heart, you've found a new life here
free of fear.
No one can threaten you tonight or any other night.
You'll learn what it is to be at ease in your life,
to be an equal and treated as well
as any servant of my lord, King Nebuchadnezzar. . . ."

[Judith's speech before Holofernes, like other untranslated passages in the following portion, is inferred.]

Judith's words enchanted Holofernes,
they were so well-measured.
All his attendants were amazed at such wisdom.
"There is not a woman in the whole world
to match this fresh intelligence
lighting up the beauty of her face."

And above the buzzing Holofernes said to her,
"God has done well
to bring you in advance of His people
into our hands, strengthening us
so we may bring a just destruction
to those so blind as to take us lightly,
having insulted my lord by refusing to kneel—
your God will right their wrongs himself
if you do as you've said,
for your words are well chosen
and you are a beautiful woman.
Your God shall live and be treated as my god,
as you will live in the palace
of King Nebuchadnezzar, so your fame
may spread through the whole world."

The fourth day after Judith arrived
Holofernes planned a private feast,
bypassing the invitations most banquets require
to all the officers, and he called in Bagoas,
his head eunuch who was taking charge of Judith,
"Talk to the Hebrew woman,
persuade her to join us for a feast.
It's disgraceful not to know her better;
everyone will laugh at us for not courting
such a beautiful woman while she's here."

When Bagoas came to Judith, he was all flattery,
"Have no fear, fair lady,
of my lord, and he will be honored
if you will come into his presence
to drink wine and be his guest
at an intimate feast
and be a chosen daughter of Assyria,
beginning to live today
like a daughter in the House of Nebuchadnezzar."

Judith was ready with an answer
"And who am I to refuse my lord?
I desire only to be of service.
Pleasing him will make me happy today
and will always be
something I will cherish until the day I die."
And so she began to dress
in the fine clothes she had brought,
in the cosmetics, jewelry and alluring perfume,
and in gentle ceremony she sent her maid ahead
to lay the soft fleeces Bagoas lent to her
on the floor in Holofernes's tent
where she would eat and then lean back.

When Judith came in and Holofernes saw her
leaning back on her fleeces,
his heart was overwhelmed
and his mind filled with desire.
From the first time he saw her,
in fact for these four days, he'd been searching
for a way to seduce her
and so he was saying, "Drink,
relax and let yourself go with us."

"I'd love to, my lord.
Today I've found a reason to live
beyond anything I've dreamed of since I was born."
Facing him, Judith ate and drank
the food her maid had brought and prepared,
and Holofernes, having accepted her reason
for being true to her God's rituals,
was disarmed at her acceptance of him
and so excited at the thought of having her,
he drank to his heart's content
until he'd poured out more wine in one night
than he'd drunk of anything in a day
since he was born.

Now, it was getting late and the staff
were leaving, tipsy, but quickly, as if they knew.
Bagoas rolled down the outside tent flap,
then dismissed the servants
(natural enough since they were exhausted)
and they went straight to sleep,
leaving Judith alone with Holofernes,
who had wound up sprawling on his bed,
his head swimming in wine.

Earlier, on the way to the feast,
Judith asked her maid not to leave
if dismissed later, but to wait outside the bedroom
just as she had done on previous mornings,
since now everyone expected her early rising
and going out for ritual prayers.
She had even reminded Bagoas and now
all had gone;
not a soul important or unimportant
was left in the bedroom.
Judith stood by Holofernes's bed,
a silent prayer in her heart:
"Lord, my God, source of all power,
have mercy on me for what my hands must do
for Jerusalem, to be a living example
of trust in Your covenant.
Now is the time to renew our heritage.
Give my plan life
to surpass the enemies,
to bring them to their knees,
who've risen up all around us,
great herds coming to devour us."

Her hand reached up
for Holofernes's well-honed sword
hanging on the front bedpost,
slung there in its jeweled scabbard.
Then, standing directly over him, swiftly
her left hand seized hold of his hair,
"Make me steel, Lord, God of Israel—today,"
as with all her strength she struck

at the nape of his neck, fiercely
and again—twice—and she pulled
his head from him,
then rolled the severed body from the bed
and tore down the royal canopy
from the bedposts.

A moment later she stepped out from the bedroom
and gave the head, wrapped in the canopy,
to her maid,
who put it in the sack she carried
with all of Judith's food and vessels.
The two women walked out together,
just as they usually did for prayer.
They passed through the camp,
walked straight across the valley,
climbed the mountain to Bethulia,
and approached the city gates.

All the women of Israel came out to see her
on the way to Jerusalem,
flushed with the victory they shared
of faith over power,
grace and daring over brute force.
Some began a dance in celebration;
Judith was carrying palm branches in her arms,
passing them to the women around her.
They were all garlanding themselves with olive,
Judith at the head of the procession
to Jerusalem, leading the women who were dancing.
And the men of Israel who were following
dressed in their armor and garlands,
songs and psalms from their lips,
lightening the feet of the dancers. . . .

The Assyrians swarmed over
the mountains in the north
with tens of thousands in armor,
gleaming in purple and gold,
hordes of infantry like rivers
flooding the valleys,

an avalanche of horsemen
pouring down on the plains.
My borders would be flames, he said,
my young men skewered on swords,
infants flung to the ground,
children seized for slaves,
and my daughters for whores.

But the Lord God has let them be outwitted
with a woman's hand.
Their hero fell
and not a young man's hand touched him;
not the sons of warrior giants,
neither a Goliath nor David,
but Judith, daughter of Merari,
stopped him in his tracks,
paralyzed his brutal power
with the beauty of her face.

And instead of fame for fleeting glamor,
she is held in honor
because she did not think of herself
but faced disaster head on,
firmly on the open path, God's way.

Persians shivered at her boldness
and Medes shuddered in terror
when they heard Judith's prayer of thanksgiving:
"Mountains may fall into the sea
and seas crack open like a broken glass of water.
Rocks may melt like wax,
but for those who live in awe of You, God,
Your presence is a steady candle,
a glowing warmth and a guide to safety."

– David Rosenberg

Chanukah in the Sixth Grade

After six years of Chanukah celebrations, the children have finally passed through the historic time when the Chanukah story took place. Not only have the sixth graders studied Greek times, but they are now immersed in the Christian era, when the story of the Maccabees was recorded.

The sixth grade can begin Chanukah by reading the story "A Syrian Diary." Here we view the story of Chanukah through the eyes of the Greeks, rather than the Jews. The sixth graders can recall last year's study of Greek life and examine it through Jewish eyes. When the class learned the Old Testament stories in third grade, they heard about a people whose lives were primarily focused on their God. The Hebrew people of that time worked the lands and did not have a strong relationship to the arts, music, or the intellect. Contrast this with the Greek approach to life. The sixth grade can brainstorm a list of reasons why the Jewish people would feel tempted to leave their own cultural background in favor of the Greek approach. The teacher can recall the *gymnasium* and how those who participated in physical and mental gymnastics were treated with great respect. The Jews were a large part of the population and already had a history of being physically enslaved. Were the Hellenized Jews trying to break free of their own religious enslavement? There are many questions that can arise in a discussion about the Hellenized Jews, and the teacher can use the eight days of Chanukah to look at the issues of assimilation. This is important for the upper school children, for they are constantly being challenged to make decisions about fitting into the adolescent society around them.

The sixth grade teacher may also choose to look at Chanukah in light of the current curriculum. The class may recall the poem "Eight Are the Lights" from second grade. Now they can recite it again, this time reflecting the sentiments of the monastic way of life. Since the story of the Maccabees has now lived with the children, the final verse can be added. This also brings an element of newness to something familiar.

The story of Hannah and her sons was also preserved during this time in history. The Jews of the Middle Ages related especially to the martyrdom of Hannah. Like the story of Judith, the story of Hannah and her sons has become part of the traditional liturgy. The class can contrast the heroism of Judith and Hannah. Hannah's martyrdom is a reflection of her times; was Judith's approach a reflection of hers? The class could write a short composition about Hannah's situation. If they were Hannah, would they encourage their sons? What are the ideals for which everyone in their own families would stand together and fight? Even though it was the sons who spoke up directly to the king, Hannah is the one who has been remembered as the heroine. Why would this be so? As the children examine Hannah's situation, the teacher might see some seeds being planted that will come to blossom when the class covers Joan of Arc. In addition to the story included here, a good poem for recitation that includes Hannah is "Let There Be Light" by Jane Yolen from her book *Milk and Honey*.[102]

Since there is so much stretching of intellectual capacities in sixth grade, the teacher might want to return to some of the more playful songs of the earlier grades. Perhaps the class can play some old favorites on their flutes or other instruments. If the sixth grade covers European geography, they might enjoy learning the Yiddish version of "Oh Hanuka." If there is a German teacher, perhaps she can help with this. The song "Chanukah/Solstice" can be sung as a way to rekindle the images of darkness and light.

Obviously, the Chanukah curriculum begins to take a turn in the upper grades. Now the tradition of intensified study can be a part of the Chanukah ritual. The older children still receive verses and stories, but now these can be vehicles for thinking and reflection, helping to prepare them for the birth of their astral forces.

Verse for Sixth Grade

EIGHT ARE THE LIGHTS
Eight are the lights
        Of Hanukkah
We light for a week
        And a day.
We kindle the lights,
        And bless the Lord,
And sing a song,
        And pray.

Eight are the lights
        Of Hanukkah
For justice and mercy
        And love,
For charity, courage
        And honor and peace,
And faith in heaven
        Above.

Eight are the lights
        Of Hanukkah
To keep ever bright
        Memories
Of the valiant soul
        And the fighting heart
And the hope of the
        Maccabees!
                – Ilo Orleans[103]

A Syrian Diary[104]

by

Joseph Halpern

It was while on a visit to a village in the West Country that I became acquainted with the local "lord of the manor." He lived in a ruined castle off the main road, and he invited me in to look at some old papers he had found in an attic. He was very patriotic and was going to give them all to his local council for their wastepaper collection. "Don't do that," I said. "there may be some valuable documents among these papers. It would be a tragedy to destroy them."

"We must all do our bit to help to win the war," he answered. "But," he added with a smile, "you're welcome to look through them and keep whatever you want."

It was fortunate that I had half an hour to spare before my bus was due to take me to the next center I had to visit. For among these old papers was a priceless document. It was written in Greek and filled about ten quarto sheets, but I had only to read a few lines to realize its importance. It was the diary of one of the personal attendants of the Syrian king Antiochus IV! This heathen had been at the court of the mad king who had tried to crush the Jewish religion at the very time that Judah the Maccabee had raised his standard of revolt. This heathen had been present at all the important interviews and conferences between Antiochus and his generals and had made a note of them in his diary. As I read, my excitement grew, and I did not notice how quickly the time was passing.

"You'll miss your bus," my host said quietly, but I was too absorbed in my reading to hear him. Three hours passed before I lifted my eyes from the document, but my face was filled with triumph.

"I am sorry I have no accommodation to put you up for the night," the lord of the manor began.

"Don't worry about me," I broke in. "I shan't be able to sleep in any case. I've made one of the finds of the century. The whole world will want to read this story of Hanukkah as told by this heathen courtier of Antiochus. It completes the picture we have from the Jewish side in the books of the Maccabees and in the Talmud. Tell me, how did such a document happen to come into your possession?"

"I've no idea. Oh, of course. A grandfather of mine visited the Middle East about eighty years ago. I remember now the bundle of papers he brought back with him. Some Arabs had sold them to him. He thought they were part of the Apocrypha, but when he showed a sheet to the authorities, they wouldn't look at it. Apparently they had been badly deceived by some previous forgeries a year or two earlier. In disgust my grandfather threw them into the attic where you found them."

Here are the first extracts. Naturally, I am translating the dates and many of the expressions into a form that you will understand. It is a private diary, and it was a good thing for the author that it never came into the hands of Antiochus.

"April 13, 167 B.C.E.

"My name is Callo, and my great-grandfather was a Greek officer in the army of Alexander the Great, may his memory be blessed. It is a pity that we have so few Greek soldiers at court now. Our king, Antiochus IV, has surrounded himself with a gang of barbarians, cowardly men from over the sea, who flatter him shamelessly. In their eyes he can do nothing wrong, and they worship him as a god. And he, like a fool, believes them. About six months ago he actually issued a decree that all his subjects should leave their own laws and become one people. Most of the subject nations readily obeyed him. It didn't matter to them what gods they worshipped, and he was vain enough to believe them when they started calling him Antiochus Epiphanes, Antiochus the man-god. But there was one people who had the pluck to refuse to obey his decree. You should have seen what happened in the throne room this morning when the reports from the provinces were read.

"Antiochus (in my circle we call him Epimanes, the Madman), beamed from ear to ear when Nicanor related how the whole of Syria from Antioch to the gates of Egypt trembled at his word. At the mention of Egypt, Antiochus's face went black. He remembered how he had been forced to turn back in his campaign against the Egyptians last year.

"But his face turned purple when Nicanor went on to say that the Jews had refused to obey his command. Apparently one of our officers had come to one of their villages and had set up an altar to Zeus. He had then called on the leading citizen, who happened to be a Jewish priest, to offer up sacrifice. Not only did the priest refuse to do this, but when another Jew came forward to offer the sacrifice, he struck him down and killed our officer (I hope he was a mercenary). Our men tried to hush up the incident, but this troublesome Jew rushed to the mountains with his five sons and started a revolt against Syria. Hundreds, some say thousands, of Jews were joining them and stern action appeared necessary.

"Antiochus was almost speechless. 'Those Jews,' he spluttered. 'How I hate them. I have pulled down the altar to their God and set up an altar to Zeus in their Temple at Jerusalem. I have burned their holy books and destroyed their finest buildings by fire. I shall not be beaten by a handful of rebels. Their religion shall perish from the earth. My will shall be done.'

" 'Hear, hear,' sang the gang of mercenaries in chorus. But we still have a few of the Greek nobility at court, and Trypho, a strapping young fellow who will make a name for himself one day, had the courage to speak up.

" 'Sire,' he cried, 'may I remind you of the way in which your illustrious ancestor Alexander treated the Jews.' (A flattering beginning in order to get Antiochus to listen to his words. Antiochus has as much right to be called a descendant of Alexander as I have—and that's none at all.)

" 'Speak on,' said the king, regaining his composure a little.

" 'Your majesty will recall. . . .' "

This was the end of the first scroll of the manuscript. The next sheet did not give the actual speech, but seemed to run on well. This is what it said:

"Trypho reminded Antiochus of the scene outside Jerusalem when Alexander's army was marching to capture it. My great-grandfather had been present, and I had often heard the story from my grandfather's lips.

"The advance guard were already rubbing their hands with glee at the prospect of looting Jerusalem, for they had heard that it was a very rich city and contained huge stores of gold and silver. Suddenly the order was given to halt. From the city a procession was approaching, more than a mile long, and all the citizens were dressed in white. At their head appeared a band of uniformed men (we later learned that they were priests) led by a young man clothed in purple garments and wearing a golden miter on his head (Simon the Just, the high priest, they called him).

"At the sight of him our Alexander stepped forward and bowed his head to the ground in worship. Our guards were speechless and thought he must have gone out of his mind. Parmenio, however, had the courage to go up to Alexander and ask why he was doing this strange thing.

"A bellow as though from a bull interrupted Trypho's story.

" 'We do not want to listen,' shouted Antiochus, 'to your old wives' tales of centuries ago. I know you are going to say that Alexander had seen this man in a dream before his conquest of Asia and that he therefore allowed the Jews to worship God in their own way. But it is all lies, lies. . . .'

"By this time Antiochus was foaming at the mouth in his frenzied fury, and Clito the chamberlain wisely told us that the royal audience was over. Only Grazi the butcher remained, and as I left I heard him dictating, in the king's name, the measures by which to put down the Jewish rebellion. I caught the words Eleazar and Hannah. Poor soul, I can imagine the torture Grazi has made ready for them. Not for nothing has he earned the title 'the Butcher.' But then he is one of the mercenary gang.

"December 7, 167 B.C.E.

"The Jewish revolt has lasted a year already. But it will soon be over. Mattathias, their leader, has just died. His five sons will probably quarrel among themselves as to who should succeed him. And that is where our chance will come. I am sorry that it may all soon lead to nothing.

"December 1, 165 B.C.E.

"Those Jews! Lysias, the viceroy, came back to Antioch today a beaten man. His was the fourth army that Antiochus had sent against them. Apparently the death of Mattathias has not weakened them. In fact, they have grown stronger and more troublesome. Their leader, Judah, must be a remarkable man. He cannot have a large army, and it is only poorly equipped. We have the resources of the world at our disposal. We have even made use of our famous corps of elephants. Yet we cannot defeat them in battle. Now that Lysias has lost Beth Sura, the road to Jerusalem is open. Will they take it? It would be funny if they recaptured their Temple on December 25, because that was the day on which Antiochus defiled it and built an altar to Zeus there three years ago. I should like to see Antiochus's face if that happens. He might think there is something in this Jewish God after all. I am beginning to think so myself.

"March 12, 164 B.C.E.

"Antiochus IV is dead. He died in Persia, and reports say that on his deathbed he confessed that all the miseries that had come upon him in the last few years were due to the fact that he had plundered the Temple of the Jews at Jerusalem and had tried to dishonor their God. I can quite believe it. The story of the miracle of oil is still being told in the bazaars at Antioch. Judah did enter the Temple on December 25 last year. The priests purified the Temple and found there a small bottle of oil with the seal still on it, which showed that it had not been touched by any gentile hands. That oil would have normally been enough for only one day. But it takes eight days to make a new supply and the Jews have a law that the perpetual lamp, once lit, must never be allowed to go out. They were worried about what to do. And then the miracle happened. That little bottle of oil burned for eight days until the new supply was ready."

I brought the manuscript to the light to see some small words at the bottom of the page, when it caught fire. The only light I had was a candle, since I was in some out-of-the-way village where electricity and gas are still considered luxuries. The parchment was so brittle and dry that in a moment nothing was left of it. What a good thing that I had translated as much as I had!

The Seven Brothers and Their Mother
The Story of Hannah 2 Maccabees 7[105]

by

Solomon Zeitlin

It happened also that seven brothers, with their mother, were arrested and tortured with whips and scorpions by the king, to compel them to partake of swine meat forbidden by the Law. One of them made himself their spokesman, and said, "What do you intend to ask and to learn from us? It is certain that we are ready to die rather than transgress the laws of our fathers."

The king in his rage ordered that pans and caldrons be heated red hot. They were heated at once, and he ordered that the tongue of the spokesman should be cut out, that they should scalp him in the Scythian manner and cut off his extremities, while the rest of his brothers and mother were looking on. When he had been reduced to a completely useless hulk, the king ordered them to bring him, while he was still breathing, to the fire, and to fry him in the fan. As the vapor from the pan grew more dense, the brothers and their mother encouraged each other to die nobly, saying, "The Lord God is watching, and in very truth will have compassion on us, just as Moses declared in his song, which bears testimony against them to their very face, saying, 'And He will have compassion upon His servants.'"

When the first one had died in this way, they brought the second to be mocked. Then they tore off his scalp by the hair and asked him, "Will you eat, or else have your body dismembered limb from limb?"

He, however, replied in the mother tongue, and said, "Never." For this reason he too underwent the same order of torture. But with his last breath he said, "You accursed wretch, you may release us from our present existence, but the King of the universe will raise us up to everlasting life because we have died for His laws."

After him the third one was brought to be mocked. When he was ordered to put out his tongue, he did so quickly. He courageously stretched forth his hands, then nobly said, "From heaven have I had these, yet because of God's laws I count them as nothing, for from Him I hope to have them back again." The king himself and his men were struck with admiration by the spirit of the young man because he minimized his sufferings.

When he too had died, they mutilated and tortured the fourth one in the same manner. As he was dying he said, "Better is it for people to be done to death by men if they have the hopeful expectation that they will again be raised up by God, but as for you, there will be no resurrection to life."

Next they brought up the fifth and treated him shamefully. As he looked at the king he said, "Because you, a finite mortal, have authority among men, you may work your will; but do not think that God has abandoned our people. You will see how His overwhelming power will torment you and your offspring."

After him they brought on the sixth. As he was about to die, he said, "Do not vainly deceive yourself. We suffer these things because of ourselves, because we sinned against our own God. That is why these astounding things have come upon us. But do not think that you will go free in thus daring to wage war against God."

Their mother was truly wonderful and is worthy of blessed memory. Though she saw her seven sons die in the space of a single day, she bore it bravely because of her faith in the Lord. She encouraged each one of them in their mother tongue, filled as she was with a noble spirit. She stirred up her womanly nature with courage, and said to them, "How you ever appeared in my womb, I do not know. It was not I who graced you with breath and life, nor was it I who arranged in order within each of you the combination of elements. It was the Creator of the World, who formed the generation of man and devised the origin of all things, and He will give life back to you in mercy, even as you now take no thought for yourselves on account of His laws."

Antiochus then thought that he was being treated contemptuously and suspected the reproachful tone in her voice. As the youngest son was still alive the king appealed to him not only by words but also by oaths, promising that he would make him both rich and envied if he would leave the ways of his fathers, that he would consider him as a friend, and would put him in an office of trust. When the young man paid no attention to him at all, the king summoned the mother and urged her to advise the lad to save himself.

After he had exhorted her for quite a while, she undertook to persuade her son. She leaned over him, and jeering at the king, she spoke in the mother tongue as follows, "My son, have pity on me, who carried you in my womb for nine months. For three years I nursed you, reared you, brought you to this stage of your life, and sustained you. I beg of you, my child, to look up to heaven and earth and see all that there is therein, and know that God did not make them out of things that were already in existence. In the same manner the human race came into being. Do not be afraid of this executioner, but show yourself worthy of your brothers. Accept death, that in God's mercy I may receive you back again along with all of your brothers."

While she was still speaking, the young man said, "What are you waiting for? I will not obey the king's command, but I will obey the command of the Law that was given to our fathers through Moses. But you, who have shown yourself to be the contriver of every evil against the Hebrews, shall not escape the hands of God. We are really suffering for our own sins. Although our living God, in order to punish and discipline us, is angry at us for a little while, He will again be reconciled with His servants.

"You profane wretch, vilest of all men, be not vainly buoyed up by your insolent, uncertain hopes, raising your hand against His servants. You have not yet escaped the judgment of the Almighty, all-seeing God. Indeed, my brothers, after enduring brief trouble, are under God's covenant for everlasting life, while you under God's judgment will receive just punishment for your arrogance. I, like my brothers, surrender body and soul for our paternal laws, invoking God speedily to be merciful to our nation, and to make you acknowledge through affliction and torment that He alone is God, while it has devolved upon me and my brothers to stay the wrath of our nation."

With this the king became furious, and dealt with him worse than with the others, bitterly resenting his sarcasm. So the seventh brother then died in purity, believing implicitly in God. Finally, after her sons, the mother also died.

Let this be enough about eating of idolatrous sacrifices and inhuman tortures.

Chanukah in the Seventh Grade

The seventh graders can acknowledge the Chanukah festival, as they did with the Days of Awe, through the Sephardic tradition. The Sephardic Jews originated in Spain and dispersed throughout many lands, most of which are covered in this year's geography study. A look at the Sephardic traditions can help create a picture of the people in those lands and the recitation of the lyrics to "Ocho Kandelikas" can bring their "voice," or language, into the classroom.

The Jews of the Sepharad maintain the tradition of oil menorahs with floating wicks. The blessing is slightly different, changing "*L'hadlik ner shel Chanukah*" to "*L'hadlik ner Chanukah.*" In some traditions the shammash is actually lit last, rather than first. It serves, then, as a light for work and reading, not as a servant to the other candles.[106]

The seventh graders may wish to make an oil menorah. The teacher can tie in the chemistry block by having the children research the properties of oil that would allow it to burn. For example, the class can experiment with a different type of vegetable oil each day. Observing and timing the flames, the children can discover which oil burns slowest, brightest, and so forth. It is said that the original oil was of olive oil base. Does the class agree that olive oil is the best carrier for Divine infusion, or would corn or canola oil burn even longer?

Another Sephardic tradition the class may enjoy is the exchange of decorated candles. According to Syrian tradition, the Shammash (leader) of the community gave decorated tapers to the Jews of the Sepharad and these tapers were used for lighting the shammash candle and the menorah each night.[107] The seventh grade can use the Stockmar decorating beeswax to make candles as gifts to the other classes to be used for lighting their menorahs. In the Sephardic tradition, Chanukah is also a time for charity. Rather than exchanging candles with each other or with family members, the children could take the candles to a retirement home or hospital.

The foods of Chanukah are different for Sephardic Jews. Instead of latkes, the oily food for the holiday is *sufganiyot*, jelly doughnuts. Along with sufganiyot, there are also *bunuelos*, which are fried fritters, similar to Mexican *churros*. The seventh graders can make these treats to eat themselves and also to share with others. Good websites for recipes are

www.epicurious.com/cooking/ holiday/hanukkah/doughnuts
and
www.boston.com/yourlife/getwrapped/recipes/bunuelos_hanukkah/

A final food idea is a potluck picnic, or *merenda*, on the last day of Chanukah. This is a tradition of the Jews who left Spain and ended up in Turkey.[108]

The teacher can relate to the class how it was the priests of the Middle Ages who preserved the story of the Maccabees, but it was the rabbis who chose to emphasize the miracle of light as the main symbol of the holiday. Why would the rabbis decide that a miracle would stir the people? Is the miracle a "wake-up call" to kindle the lights of our spirit, as the shofar reminds us in the fall? In what ways does something miraculous affect people? Here the teacher can tie in the Wish, Wonder and Surprise block. As a follow-up activity the class can look at copies of the poems about the Chanukah miracle and then write their own poems about miracles or the images of Chanukah.

The story chosen for seventh grade, "A Secret Chanukah," takes place during the Inquisition. Even if the class has not yet covered the Age of Exploration, its telling is still appropriate at this time. In this story there is an emphasis on inner light, and it contains imagery that speaks to Christmas and Advent as well as to Chanukah. Not only is it a story for the season but it also speaks to the soul qualities needed in the twelve-year-old. As Torin Finser once said in a class discussion, "The seventh grade curriculum matches the children's feelings of 'being at sea.'" During this holiday season we can remind them that the beacon of light which brings them safely to shore is actually kindling within them.

Verses for Seventh Grade

OCHO KANDELIKAS

    Hanuka linda sta aki
    Ocho kandelikas para mi
    O . . . Una kandelika . . .
    Dos kandelikas
    Tres kandelikas
    Kuatro kandelikas
    Sinko kandelikas
    Seis kandelikas
    Siete kandelikas
    Ocho kandelikas para mi.

    Michas fiestas vo fazer
    Kun alegriyas I plazer
    O . . . Una kandelika . . .
    Dos kandelikas
    Tres kandelikas
    Kuatro kandelikas
    Sinko kandelikas
    Seis kandelikas
    Siete kandelikas
    Ocho kandelikas para mi.

    Los pastelikos vo kumer
    kun almendrikas I la myel
    O . . . Una kandelika . . .
    Dos kandelikas
    Tres kandelikas
    Kuatro kandelikas
    Sinko kandelikas
    Seis kandelikas
    Siete kandelikas
    Ocho kandelikas para mi.
        – Flory Jagoda[109]

HANUKKAH LIGHTS

I kindle my eight little candles,
My Hanukkah candles, and lo!
Visions and dreams half-forgotten
Come back of the dim long ago.

I musingly gaze at my candles,
And see in their quivering flames
Written fiery letters,
Immortal indelible names,

The names of valorous Hebrews
Whose soul no sword could subdue;
A battlefield stretches before me,
Where many are conquered by few.

Defeated lies Syria's army,
Judea's proud foe, in the field;
And Judah, the great Maccabeus,
I see in his helmet and shield.

His eyes are like stars in the desert,
Like music each resonant word:
"We fought and we conquered the tyrant,
For People and Towns of the Lord!"

He speaks, and the hills are repeating,
"For People and Towns of the Lord."
The groves and the towers echo,
"For People and Towns of the Lord."

Swiftly the message is spreading,
Judea, Judea is free!
The lamp in the Temple rekindled,
And banished idolatry!

My eight little candles expire,
Around me spreads darkness of night,
But deep in my soul is still burning
The ages-old miracle light.

— Philip M. Raskin[110]

A Secret Chanukah[111]

by

Peninnah Schram

Once, in the dark days of King Ferdinand and Queen Isabella of Spain, there lived a young girl named Francisca. Fate was not kind to her, for of all times in which to be born, she was born in Spain during the misery of the Inquisition. It was an age of great evil and persecution. For years Jews who observed their holidays, or sought God in prayer, or endeavored to teach their children the heritage of their ancestors were imprisoned and often executed upon a burning stake.

In August of 1492, Francisca had stood upon the dock and watched as the great Christopher Columbus set sail for the New World. She had longed to go with him and escape her life of suffering. She prayed for someone to rescue her and all the other secret Jews. Perhaps, she thought, in the New World things were different. Could it be that the New World was really God's Garden of Eden, a paradise where there were no Inquisitors and where people loved one another? Francisca had remained on the dock long after the *Niña*, the *Pinta*, and the *Santa Maria* had left the harbor. She watched each of the ships sail out to sea and slowly disappear into the horizon. Even when she could no longer see the huge white sails filled with the ocean breeze, she continued to gaze out over the blue waters.

Now it was winter. Kislev had come to the world. Francisca and her family knew it was time for Chanukah, but they also knew that if they were caught lighting the *chanukiah* they could be imprisoned, or worse.

One night, toward the very end of the month of Kislev, Francisca lay asleep in her bed. A brilliant moon visited the world that night and three stars appeared in the sky above the town. A breeze stirred, and softly tapped at the shutters to Francisca's window. Gently, it loosened the latch and the shutters swung open. The breeze floated through the room and stroked Francisca's face with its cool touch. It beckoned to Francisca to ride its invisible wave to lands far away.

Francisca was not sure she wished to embark on such a nocturnal journey, but the breeze was persistent, and finally she agreed. Up, up she rose and floated out the window.

For just a moment, she hovered over the town, marveling at the stillness in the streets. All the houses were dark. No one moved. Cats called to one another. Night birds sang their quiet songs.

Then, in an instant, Francisca found herself soaring through the skies. She flew over towns, over tall mountains, and through wide valleys. As she passed one of the mountaintops, she reached down to scoop up some snow from the peak.

On and on she traveled on the back of the wind. How free she felt! She soared like a bird. For half the night, she flew. Then finally the wind began to calm down and Francisca floated softly down to earth. She landed just outside the mouth of a deep, dark cave.

Gently, the breeze pushed Francisca inside the cave. For several moments, she could not see at all. It was as black as the blackest of nights, but somehow she did not bump into anything even once. After a while, she came to a room deep inside the cave. In the middle of the room there was a fire burning, and around the fire, sitting on thrones, were five figures dressed in robes, their faces hidden from view by their hoods.

"Francisca, the breeze has brought you to us," said one of the figures.

"We have heard your prayers," said another.

"We have a gift for you," said a third.

Then they removed their hoods. The glow of the fire filled their eyes and, even though it was very dark in the cave, it was easy to see each of the five men.

Francisca was astonished.

"I am Judah Maccabee," said the first man. "Next to me sit my four brothers. God has given us the task of tending this fire. It is a special flame kindled by a spark from the Divine throne. It is the light of God. Those who are comforted by its warmth find courage and hope."

Francisca gazed at the crackling flame. She could feel its warmth.

"When we first began our struggle against the tyrant Antiochus," said Judah, "we hid from his soldiers in caves. One night, after a battle, we sat in a cave nursing all our comrades who had been wounded in the day's fighting. It was cold in the cave and dark. No matter how we tried, we could not keep the wind from putting out our fire. That night, for the first and only time, I wondered if we could actually prevail. Could we defeat the most powerful army in the world? Then I remembered the words from the Torah: '*Mi Chamocha Baelim Adonai?* Who is like our God among all of the false gods of the other nations?' Those words gave me courage. They gave me strength. I knew at that moment that if we believed in the power of Adonai, our God, we would win. Suddenly, our sputtering flame rose and roared. No matter how hard the wind blew that night, the flame continued to burn. The fire was so bright and warm, it made us all feel brave. After that night, we were never fearful again. The next day, we defeated Antiochus's army and recaptured the Temple."

Judah stopped speaking and walked toward Francisca. He placed his hands on her shoulders and looked deeply into her eyes. "We know that you and your family cannot kindle the lights of the chanukiah this year. Do not be sad, and do not despair. Turn to the flames, Francisca, and study them well."

Francisca watched the flames rise and fall. She studied every part of their dance. She memorized the reds, oranges, yellows, whites, and blues that appeared in the fire. She followed every spark that flew out and disappeared into the dark night.

"Now close your eyes," whispered Judah. "Can you still see the flame in your mind?"

Francisca nodded her head. She did not dare speak for fear that her voice would shatter the magic of this moment.

"God's light will always be with you. When you are frightened or sick at heart, all you need to do is close your eyes and find God's light. Tonight is the fourth night of Chanukah. When you are alone in your room and three stars have appeared in the sky, close your eyes and find the lights of God's fire. Feel its warmth. Feel your courage. Then imagine that you have your family's chanuklah before you. Take hold of the shammash and thrust it into God's fire. Use this flame to light the four candles in your chanukiah. This is your secret. No one can ever take this flame from you. It will always be there for you whenever you need hope or courage."

A gust of wind blew through the shutters and lifted the covers from Francisca's sleeping body and awakened her. She shivered. She was no longer in the cave with the Maccabees. Here she was back in her bed. Had she been dreaming?

The moon was shining and spreading its soft white glow over the surface of the street outside. Stars twinkled and sparkled. Then she remembered about the flame. She closed her eyes and the flame appeared just as Judah had said it would. She imagined her family's chanukiah with the shammash in its place and four other candles standing tall, awaiting their kindling flame.

Francisca used the flame to kindle her chanukiah. Then she opened her eyes and looked at the stars once more. What if her evening's adventure had really been a dream? No matter, she thought. God's light is very real. This Chanukah, she knew she had been given a secret gift. One that she would keep forever.

Chanukah in the Eighth Grade

In eighth grade the children will finally engage in a study of the Chanukah story itself. So far the actual historical account has not been told in the classroom. Instead, in the earlier grades, the students have learned stories, poems, songs, games and traditions relating to the whole Chanukah experience.

Eighth grade history covers revolutions. Appropriately, the battle that inspired the story of Chanukah is sometimes considered the first guerilla revolt in recorded history. Having absorbed background information for years now, the eighth graders can analyze this story from many angles. Let them consider first the original event of the war, which is Mattathias's attack on a fellow Jew, a Hellenized Jew. Only after Mattathias killed the other man did the soldiers respond. The impetus for fighting came from within the Jewish community. Can the eighth grade find other revolutionary stories where the fighting began with a division from within, rather than against a larger power? The contrast between the American Revolution as opposed to the Civil War might be an appropriate example. The teacher can help the children look at the Chanukah story as an example of the "Divide and Conquer" theory, but the unique aspect of this story is that, despite division, the Jews were not conquered.

Although the Maccabees are the heroes of the story, the eighth graders should consider the shadow side of their victory. The Maccabees had Greek names—Mattathias, Judah, Jonas—not Hebrew names. Clearly they had acculturated themselves somewhat into Greek society, living with less loyalty to their heritage than the rabbis, but more loyalty than the Hellenized Jews. Here a band of a few men was able to gain freedom, it seemed, for all of the people. However, history teaches that the Maccabees ended up abusing their control and because of this, their rule over the people lasted less than one hundred years. The Jews who believed in the power of the spirit, rather than of force, were the ones who remained the leaders of the Jewish people.

The eighth graders can look at where else in history small groups have instigated great wars. Where else in history have good intentions spoiled with the rush of power? In modern history the class can look at the Cuban revolution as a modern day Chanukah story. They could also discuss religious freedom and why so many wars have occurred in the name of religion. Is this the spirit of religion or contrary to it?

    So, if the Maccabees themselves did not remain in power, why has this holiday prevailed? The class can discuss how the Jewish people have been a persecuted people since their earliest days. The class could be reminded that enslaved Jews built the pyramids. Yet as much as they have been enslaved, expelled and tortured, the Jewish people have endured. The class can recall the other peoples they have studied throughout the years—the Babylonians, the Greeks and even the early Romans—whose traditional ways of life and beliefs did not carry over into modern times. Why have the Jews been able to maintain their cultural and religious practices? The class can then see that the true miracle of Chanukah is not that the oil lasted for eight days, but that the Jewish people have survived the changing epochs with much of their culture intact.

    The eighth graders, living with revolutions and reflecting on the different elements within this story, should plan on presenting it at the winter assembly. I have included a version of the story in this guide, but the teacher may prefer to assign a simple research project for the class and have the students practice their library skills by finding different versions of the Chanukah story. The class can then compare and contrast what they find and decide how best to bring the story to the rest of the children in the school. They might write a short play, learn a poetic verse, or take turns telling parts of the story. They become the shammash for the rest of the school. This can become a school tradition, giving the younger grades something to look forward to each year, as they listen to the uppr class students and then finally take over this responsibility themselves.

    An eighth grade activity for Chanukah can be dreidel making. Now, in light of geometry, the class can make wood or clay models. The dreidel is a combination of a cube and a pyramid, both of which are challenging forms in clay! This is yet another way of allowing the symbols to grow in the imagination of the children. The lesson could be done in such a way that the class does not know they are making a dreidel until the work is almost completed. This would bring in the element of surprise, something the ofttimes-jaded eighth grader might need.

The eighth grade can also listen to Handel's oratorio, *Judah Maccabeus*. Handel composed it in the eighteenth century, so it is relevant to the time frame of the eighth grade curriculum. The class can take parts from the oratorio, such as "See, the Conqu'ring Hero Comes," and sing them in chorus or play them in orchestra.

Another idea is inspired by a torch relay that happens every year in Israel between Modin and Jerusalem. The eighth grade could have their own "torch relay" at the school, though with some adaptations. First of all, I recommend that this activity occur during main lesson when there is less activity about the building. Also, be sure to tell support staff when this will be taking place. The teacher or class parent(s) places candles in various spots around the school and write clues for each place. The first student in the class is given the shammash and the first clue. This student goes out to find the unlit candle and lights it with the shammash. He or she then returns to the classroom with the clue that was under the candle and hands it and the shammash to the next student, who ventures out to light the next candle. This continues for as many children as there are in the class. The children waiting in the room should be busy with work. The passing off of the shammash should happen in silence. When the last child returns, the whole class walks the entire route of candles. They must remember their initial order so that they can take turns leading from one candle to another.

As they walk, the class can sing one of the quieter Chanukah songs. The candles could either be left in place or gathered as the children progress, so that they become a menorah themselves, carrying the light of Chanukah throughout the buildings or the grounds. When the class returns to the room, the teacher can complete the cycle by lighting a candle in honor of the whole class. This could be followed by the class reciting together the poem "Light One Candle for the Maccabee Children," which would tie their individual experiences to a greater relationship with the world.

Verses for Eighth Grade

THE TALE OF HANUKKAH
RETOLD BY THIS GAY MINSTREL'S PEN OF GOLD

An ancient king is known to us,
Who bore the name Antiochus.
Of all the knaves and fools of yore
Who e'er that lofty title bore,
Who loved to strut and kill and quarrel,
He took the palm, the wreath, the laurel.
(You'll hear of this unpleasant creature
Some day from your classroom teacher.)

Now first the king was proven foolish
When, in his regal way and mulish,
He loudly called himself a god,
For worship by the common clod.
And all the courtiers bowed low
Before his braggadocio—
A profitable, harmless thing
It is to please one's doting king.

He set his statues everywhere
And ordered men to worship there.
To busts of metal and of stone
The zealous populace fell prone,
While in the squares the soldiers stood—
A cheery, joyous brotherhood—
To pierce with pike the luckless gent
Who failed to hail the monument.

But here and there appeared a Jew,
A member of that stubborn crew
Whom even kings of high degree
Could never force to bend the knee.
"One only God is ours!" they cried—
A God that none of them had spied.
Yet from this Being far and strange
Not threat of death would make them change.

The king was wroth. "I stand supreme
O'er gods and men. These Jews blaspheme!
Go, set my image in the place
Of worship of this willful race.
Defile their sacred objects. Give
Them pork—who eats not shall not live!
And so they did. Too, in their spite
They dimmed the everlasting light.

In Modin town the news was spread,
Where ancient Mattathias led
His five great sons and all the rest
In homage to the Being Blest.
He smote one treacherous coward down
And called the men of Modin town
To fight the king and all his men
And purify their shrine again.

Heading the Maccabean breed,
The mighty Judah took the lead.
Throughout the land the fighters came,
Their arms held high, their hearts aflame.
A handful many thousands slew!
They hacked the Syrian army through,
Until the Maccabean stand
Had saved our altars and our land.

Then, in the Temple's walls they fell
On one day's oil—which, strange to tell,
They saw give holy fire for eight!—
A wonder which we celebrate
As Hanukkah this very day,

Telling the world, and kings, for aye—
No matter what you scheme or do,
You simply cannot crush the Jew!
— Abraham Burstein[112]

LIGHT ONE CANDLE
>Light one candle for the Maccabee children
>>with thanks that their light did not die.
>Light one candle for the pain they endured
>>when their right to exist was denied.
>Light one candle for the terrible sacrifice
>>justice and freedom demand.
>But, light one candle for the wisdom to know
>>when the peacemaker's time is at hand.

>*Refrain:*
>>Don't let the light go out,
>>It's lasted for so many years.
>>Don't let the light go out,
>>>Let it shine through our love and our tears.

>Light one candle for the strength that we need
>>to never become our own foe.
>Light one candle for those who are suffering
>>the pain we learned long ago.
>Light one candle for all we believe in.
>>Let anger not tear us apart,
>And light one candle to bind us together
>>with peace as a song in our heart.

>*Refrain*

>What is the memory that's valued so highly
>>that we keep it alive in that flame?
>What's the commitment to those who have died
>>when we cry out they've not died in vain?
>We have come this far always believing
>>that justice will somehow prevail.
>This is the burden and this is the promise
>>and this is why we will not fail.

>*Refrain*
>—a song by Peter Yarrow (of Peter, Paul & Mary)[113]

A Teaching by Rabbi Avi Weiss[114]

Needing oil for eight days but having found oil that could last for only one, most people would not have lit the Temple candelabra at all. Why light when failure is certain? Why make the effort if the effort is doomed? The miracle of the first day is that the Maccabees found the inner strength, the inner courage, to light the menorah in the first place. They did not give up, for nothing is impossible, and in the end they prevailed.

No one is immune from feeling loneliness, from moments of darkness and night. But . . . light can remove darkness, day follows night. The message of Hanukkah is to kindle the first light: to care, to be concerned and to lift others. "In the end," the Hasidic masters said, "a little bit of light has the power to drive away the darkness."

How Chanukah Came to Be[115]

by

Peninnah Schram

More than two thousand years ago, there lived a powerful but wicked king of Syria whose name was Antiochus. Antiochus ruled an enormous empire of many different lands. One of these countries was the entire land of Israel. There is a saying that "the ways of the wicked are like deep darkness," and this was certainly true of Antiochus, for he was so mean and cruel that he made it a very dark time, a scary time, and a sad time for everyone who lived in his kingdom.

Antiochus thought he was a god, so he ordered statues of himself to be placed in every town in the land. He wanted people to bow down to his statue and worship him with all the other Greek gods. If the people refused, he would order his soldiers to take their swords and kill them right there on the spot. The only religion that was allowed now was the religion of Antiochus.

Imagine—there could be no more Jewish holidays, no more Jewish celebrations, no more Jewish Temple in Jerusalem. As his first order, Antiochus commanded that the great Temple, the Temple built by King Solomon and dedicated to God, be destroyed. He ordered his soldiers to tear it apart, to burn the Torah scrolls, to destroy the old Ark, and in its place, to erect a statue of Antiochus.

One day, Antiochus's soldiers came to a small town not far from Jerusalem called Modin. Many faithful Jews lived there. The soldiers rode big black horses and brought gigantic carts with them. In the carts were statues of Antiochus. The soldiers lifted the statues out of the carts and began to place them all around the town. The people of Modin gathered around the carts to see what the soldiers were doing. The captain of the guards announced to them: "Antiochus orders all the people in Modin to assemble tomorrow morning in the center of town. You will bring gifts to the god Antiochus and bow down to his statues. You will kiss the feet of his statues and take an oath to worship him."

When the Jews in Modin heard this, they became worried. "What shall we do?" they cried. "We are Jews! We have only one God: the God of Abraham, Isaac and Jacob, the God who gave us the Torah. We cannot worship other gods. But if we refuse, the soldiers will kill us."

The next day, everyone in Modin came to the center of town. The soldiers were there, sharpening their swords. The captain called out his orders: "Everyone line up! Line up before your new god, Antiochus!"

The Jews did as they were told.

"You there," called out the captain. "You are the first in line. Come up here and kiss the feet of the god Antiochus."

Slowly, the first person in line came forward. But just as he did, a man ran in front of him and blocked his way. It was Mattathias, one of God's priests.

"No Jew will ever bow down to an idol," Mattathias declared. "Our God is not Antiochus. We have only one God, and we will not let you take away our holidays, our rituals, and our Temple."

Mattathias stood right in front of the captain as he spoke. His words made the captain turn red with anger and shake with rage. The captain seized his sword to slay Mattathias, but Mattathias swiftly pulled a knife from under his robe and stabbed the captain first.

"Let all who want to fight the evil Antiochus follow me!" shouted Mattathias as he ran through the town. And before Antiochus's guards knew what was happening, Mattathias had escaped with his sons and other Jews.

Antiochus was enraged when he heard what had happened in Modin. "Who does this Mattathias think he is?" he barked. "Does he think he can defy me? I will teach him never to disobey me again."

So Antiochus sent a troop of soldiers to find Mattathias and throw him in prison. But Mattathias was hard to find. He and his followers were hiding in the caves of the Judean hillside, which they knew so well. Their small group was led by one of Mattathias's five sons, Judah, who was a very clever leader. Whenever Antiochus's soldiers passed by, Judah and his men would leap from their hiding places and jump on the soldiers and shout, "There is no God like our God!" With all their heavy armor, shields, and spears, the soldiers could move only very slowly, and by the time they recovered from the surprise attack, Judah and his men would have disappeared back into the hills.

As word spread of Judah and his group, they came to be known as the Maccabees, meaning "hammers," because they pounced on their enemies like a hammer hits a nail, and then before their foes knew what had hit them, Judah and his band would be gone.

Antiochus tried many times to defeat the Maccabees, but each time Judah outsmarted him and won the battle. Finally, Antiochus knew he was defeated. He had lost too many good soldiers. So Antiochus took what remained of his armies away from the land of Judea. The Maccabees had won!

Though Antiochus was gone, the signs of his fury remained. He had destroyed so many things in Judea. He had ruined many Jewish towns. He had put up his statues everywhere. He had defiled the old Temple in Jerusalem.

Judah Maccabee and his men wept when they saw what had been done to the old Temple. There was garbage everywhere. Pigs and other animals had been sacrificed on the altar. The beautiful curtains around the Ark had been ripped and slashed. The Torah scrolls lay torn and burned. The Ner Tamid had been extinguished. And in the middle of the sanctuary lay the Temple's magnificent menorah, overturned, with all the oil spilled from its cups.

Judah Maccabee suddenly sounded a series of blasts on his trumpet. "Ta, ta! Ta, ta! Ta, ta!"

"Look what I have found," called Judah. In his hand was a small jar. "It is oil," he said, "the pure oil that our priests used to light the great menorah. There is not very much inside, but we will use what we have."

He moved to the menorah and set it upright. Carefully, he poured the oil into one of its cups and lit the wick. A beautiful flame arose. It flickered, and then it glowed. The Maccabees were inspired by the sign of the flame burning in the menorah again.

"God is here with us," said Judah. "This is God's flame, and this Temple is God's house. Let us make it fit for God to visit again."

Judah and his men worked very hard to clean up the Temple. They polished the silver cups and candlesticks. The pulled the weeds from the earthen floor. They washed the walls and the floors, mended the curtains and rebuilt the Ark. This took them many days, and all the while, as they worked to clean the Temple, the flame in the menorah continued to burn. The flame burned for eight days. No one thought it would last for more than a few hours—maybe a day at the most. The Maccabees wondered at this flame lasting so long. There was only the oil from one small jar. But a miracle occurred and the flame burned for eight days. It kept them company, as if God were working alongside them.

Finally, on the twenty-fifth day of the month of Kislev, 165 C.E., the Temple was finished and rededicated to God. It had been prepared so God could visit again. That is what Chanukah means.

This made the Maccabees so happy that they celebrated the miracle of the oil and the rededication of the Temple for eight days. Who would have thought that the flame would burn for so long? But then who would have thought that a small group of courageous Jews could win such a battle for freedom against the powerful armies of Antiochus?

Chanukah Candle Blessing

Traditional

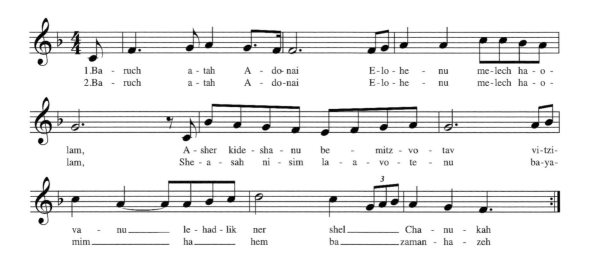

1. Baruch atah Adonai Elohenu melech haolam, Asher kideshanu bemitzvotav vitzivanu lehadlik ner shel Chanukah
2. Baruch atah Adonai Elohenu melech haolam, Sheasah nisim laavotenu bayamim hahem bazaman hazeh

Kindle the Taper

Emma Lazarus   Jacob Singer

Kindle the taper like the steadfast star Ablaze on evening's forehead o'er the earth; Send thro' the night its luster till afar, An eightfold splendor shine above thy hearth.

(Goodman, *The Hanukkah Anthology*, p. 423)

196

Chag Ha-Or

Words and music by teachers,
College of Jewish Studies, 1975

1. I feel the warm candles glow As we stand so near, The flames are dancing in a row, Cha-nu-kah, Cha-nu-kah is here.
2. We think about the Mac-ca-bees, As we stand so near, They helped to keep our peo-ple free, Cha-nu-kah, Cha-nu-kah is here.

Chag, chag, chag ha-or, chag ha-or, chag ha-or.
Chag, chag, chag ha-or, chag ha-or.

(Saypol, *My Very Own Chanukah Book*, p. 26)

Oh Hanuka — Yiddish Version

M. Riverman Folk Song

Oy Ha-nu-kah, Oy Ha-nu-kah, a yom-tov a she-ner, A lus-ti-ker, a fre-le-kher, ni-to nokh a zoi-ner, Al-le nakht in dreid-lekh sh'pi-len mir, Zi-dik he-se lat-kes est on a shir. Ge-shvin-der, tzindt kin-der, Di di-nin-ke likh-te-lekh ohn. Zingt "Al ha-ni-sim," loibt Gott far di-ni-sim, un kumt gi-kher tan-tzen in kohn. kumt gi-kher tan-tzen in kohn.

(Coopersmith, *The New Jewish Songbook*, p. 30)

Oh Hanuka – Hebrew Version

E. Indelman   Folk Song

(Coopersmith, *The New Jewish Songbook*, p. 30)

Oh Hanuka

F. Minkoff
Folk Song

Alternate English verse:

Oh Hanukah, Oh Hanukah, come light the menorah.
Let's have a party, we'll all dance the Hora.
Gather round the table, we'll give you a treat,
Dreidles to play with and good things to eat.
And while we are playing, the candles are burning low,
One for each night, they shed a sweet light,
To remind us of days long ago.
One for each night, they shed a sweet light,
To remind us of days long ago.

CHANUKAH
RECORDER DUET

(Burakoff, *Let's Play*)

HANUKKAH

L. Kipnis   Folk

Ha - nu - kah   Ha - nu - kah   fest - i - val   of   light   Ha - nu - kah
Ha - nu - kah   Ha - nu - kah   hag   ya - feh   kol   kakh,   Or   ha - viv

Ha - nu - kah   can - dles   bur - ning   bright   Ha - nu - kah   Ha - nu - kah
mi - sa - viv,   gil   l'   ye - led   rah.   Ha - nu - kah   Ha - nu - kah

drei - dles   spin   and   turn   spin   and   turn   spin   and   turn   while   the   can - dles   burn.
s'   vi - von   sov,   sov,   sov,   sov,   sov,   sov,   sov,   ma   na - im   va - tov.

(Goodman, *The Hanukkah Anthology*, p. 419)

My Drëdl

S.S. Grossman S.E. Goldfarb

It has a lovely body
With legs so short and thin:
And when it is all tired,
It drops and then I win.

O drëdl, drëdl, drëdl,
With legs so short and thin:
O drëdl, drëdl, drëdl,
It drops and then I win.

My drëdl is always playful
It loves to dance and spin:
A happy game of drëdl,
Come play, now let's begin.

O drëdl, drëdl, drëdl,
It loves to dance and spin:
O drëdl, drëdl, drëdl,
Come play, now let's begin.

(Coopersmith, *The New Jewish Songbook*, p. 23)

MI Y'MALEL
WHO CAN RETELL? (ROUND)

B.M. Edidin Adapted by M. Ravina

(Coopersmith, *The New Jewish Songbook*, pp.32–33)

Shalom Haverim
Israeli Four Part Round

Traditional

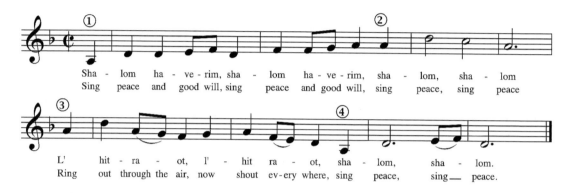

Sha - lom ha - ve - rim, sha - lom ha - ve - rim, sha - lom, sha - lom
Sing peace and good will, sing peace and good will, sing peace, sing peace

L' hit - ra - ot, l' hit - ra - ot, sha - lom, sha - lom.
Ring out through the air, now shout ev - ery where, sing peace, sing peace.

(Coopersmith, *The New Jewish Songbook*, p. 180)

S'vivon

L. Kipnis Folk Song

S' - vi - von, sov, sov, sov, Ha - nu - ka hu hag tov!
Ha - nu - ka hu hag tov! S' - vi - von, sov, sov, sov
Hag sim - ha hu la - am nes ga - dol ha - ya sham!
Nes ga - dol ha - ya sham! hag sim - ha hu la - am

Little Dreidle spin, spin, spin, Hanuka is a day of joy!
Great was the miracle that happened there.

(Coopersmith, *The New Jewish Songbook*, p. 25)

Mo'oz Tsur
Rock of Ages

Liturgy   Eng. verse: M. Jastrow

Mo - oz tsur y' - shu - o - si, l'ho no - e l' - sha - bë - ah
Rock of A - ges, let our song Praise Thy sav - ing pow - er.

Ti - kon bës t' - fi - lo - si, v'shom to - do n'za - bë - ah
Thou, a - midst the rag - ing foes, Wast our shelt - ring tow - er.

L'es to - hin mat - be - ah mi tsor ha m'na - be - ah
Fu - rious, they as - sailed us. But Thine arm a - vailed us

Oz eg - mor b' - shir miz - mor, ha - nu - kas ha - mizr be - ah.
And Thy word broke their sword When our own strength failed us.

(Coopersmith, *The New Jewish Songbook*, p. 28)

Once an Evil King (Round)

H. Reinstein   H. Coopersmith

Once an e - vil king did reign, our ho - ly Tem - ple did pro - fane, An -
Then rose Ju - dah, he - ro great, and saved the peo - ple from sad fate. O

ti - o - chus, An - ti - o - chus, An - ti - o - chus, An - ti - o - chus
Ju - dah, Ju - dah Mac - ca - bee, O Ju - dah, Ju - dah Mac - ca - bee.

(Coopersmith, *The New Jewish Songbook*, p. 32)

Chanukah/Solstice

Linda Hirschhorn

Turning, Turning, spirit yearning reaching for the night, colors going shadows growing, darkening the light ancient story told, renewed with the cold, mystery of light burnt into the night.

(Shabbat Shenit Study Group, 1991)

SEE, THE CONQU'RING HERO COMES

George F. Handel

(Goodman, *The Hanukkah Anthology*, pp. 426–427)

Conclusion

America is a melting pot, and there is a trend in public and private education to teach the children about our global village. Waldorf education has within the pedagogy a multicultural approach that is truly unique. The children in a Waldorf school learn through stories, biographies, songs, geography and many other disciplines. They do not learn about the "concept" of African history and civilization, rather they experience living pictures. Many Waldorf graduates have expressed the sentiment that their education enabled them to interact successfully with people from all over the world.

Waldorf schools arise through the impetus within a community, and a lot of pioneering effort is involved in bringing a school to realization. Each school must strive to be a true reflection of the community that creates it, and people should feel that their individual religious beliefs are supported and visible in both the curricula and the festival life of the school. No particular religion should dominate the outer form of the school.

Waldorf education is an "education towards freedom" as well as "creativity in education." The American schools in particular seem to be re-examining the true meaning of these expressions and exciting new impulses are occurring. Steiner created a dynamic pedagogy that has withstood the tests of time, and we in a new millennium are challenged to use our creative forces of intuition and inspiration to meet what our times present to us. It is the responsibility of the faculty to better educate the parents as to how the Waldorf curriculum carries multiculturalism at its very foundation. It is also the faculty's responsibility to penetrate even deeper into Steiner's indications. Through study and meditations we can continually find ways to bring the fruits of Steiner's indications forward with integrity of purpose. For the truth is that all people are represented in the curriculum. If families feel alienated, regardless of why, the faculty needs to figure out what they are doing to mistakenly perpetuate the myth that Waldorf schools are elitist. When this is taken up as a faculty, there is a healing force that begins to penetrate the whole school, much like in a child study.

This book is not a conclusion, but rather a beginning. I have only touched upon three of the major Jewish holidays. What I have discovered in the course of writing and teaching is how easily the curriculum naturally lends itself to the inclusion of other multicultural festivals and traditions. More work is being done within our teaching community to explore the additional worldly pieces of the curriculum, such as in Betty Staley's wonderful book on Africa, *Hear the Voice of the Griot*.

Everything takes time and energy. Teachers can be the ones to take on the task of evolving the curriculum. They have a wealth of knowledge and training, both practical and pedagogical, that can unify different streams of experience. As more individuals of different backgrounds and cultures find their way into Waldorf teaching, there will be many more "microcosms" within our community.

Often teachers find colleagues with similar backgrounds and work together. This could take place at regional and national conferences, stimulating wonderful discussions that can then be shared with the larger group. Our teaching community can be a wealth of information when we look into our own heritage and bring pictures to each other out of what we know. This process of multiculturalizing may inspire other members of the school community who wish to share their traditions with the larger community. I suggest that a teacher serve as an advisor to any family or families wanting to engage in a research project like this one. A grounding in anthroposphical Spiritual Science is integral to helping include different traditions as living pictures for the students.

In my own experience as a Jewish person, I have "bumped up against some walls" regarding the festivals. I have come to see that the walls are not a living reality but were there because of my preconceived notions. If the school takes the time to educate and listen to the parents, the school can then serve as a guide not only to the outer dimensions of the festivals, but also to the universal within the festivals. When we are able to share with the families the universal truths from both anthroposophy and that which the parents bring to the school, then we will truly be on our way to creating a global village. It is through this type of dialogue that each person can be seen as an image of the Christ Being, where Christ does not stand for a particular dogma, but for love and compassion. This, after all, is the essential education that all parents want for their children, and it forms the core of Waldorf education.

Appendix 1
High Holiday and Chanukah Dates

Holiday	2008	2009	2010	2011	2012	2013
Erev Rosh Hashanah	9/29	9/18	9/8	9/28	9/16	9/4
Rosh Hashanah	9/30	9/19	9/9	9/29	9/17	9/5
Erev Yom Kippur	10/8	9/27	9/17	10/7	9/25	9/13
Yom Kippur	10/9	9/28	9/18	10/8	9/26	9/14
First Night of Chanukah	12/21	12/11	12/1	12/20	12/22	11/27
Last Night of Chanukah	12/28	12/18	12/8	12/27	12/29	12/4

SOURCE: JewishGen society. Conversion Calendar: Jewish festival dates. http://www.jewishgen.org/jos/josfest.htm

Appendix 2

Selected Sources for Jewish Books and Judaica

A.R.E. Publishing
3945 South Oneida Street, Denver, CO 80237 (800) 346-7779
This is an excellent source for Jewish music for children, both in recorded format and songbooks. It also supplies good craft books and plays for various ages.

Behrman House Catalog
235 Watchung Avenue, West Orange, NJ 07052 (800) 221-2755
This catalog is primarily for Jewish educators, but non-Jewish teachers may find the teachers' guides and the curriculum sources easier to understand and use than the adult texts on Jewish holidays.

Jonathan David Co.
68-22 Eliot Avenue, Middle Village, NY 11379 (718) 456-8611
This catalog company offers a wide assortment of texts on Jewish themes. Their children's category is not very large, but the books chosen seem to be among the top choices on the market. A good reference catalog to have on hand

Museum of Tolerance
9786 West Pico Blvd., Los Angeles, CA 90035 (800) 553-4474
The catalog for this museum is devoted solely to Judaica, or Jewish artifacts. While some of the prices are high end, there are menorahs, shabbat candleholders, and dreidels that might be within the range of a classroom budget.

The Source for Everything Jewish
P.O. Box 48836, Niles, IL 60714-0836 (800) 426-2567
This catalog lives up to its name! It has books, art, artifacts, food, toys and more, at reasonable prices. Recommended over the Museum of Tolerance catalog

Union of American Hebrew Congregations (UAHC) Catalog
(800) 212-650-4121
This catalog lists mostly texts for Jewish educators, but there may be some listings in the fiction section that older classes could read or keep in the classroom library.

www.hebcal.com/holidays
This website lists the Torah portions that are commonly read on the various Jewish holidays. These passages might be of interest to the third grade teacher in particular, but also for teachers who wish to deepen their understanding of the relationships between Judaism and anthroposophy by reading Steiner's interpretations of these passages.

In addition to the above sources, numerous other interesting and reliable resources are available on the Internet by typing the holiday names into your search engine.

Appendix 3

Permissions

The following authors and publishers have generously given permission to use material from their works.

"Sing Along Song" by Steve Reuben from *Especially Wonderful Days* ©1976 A.R.E. Publishing. Used by permission.

"Rosh Hashanah" by Ben Aronin from *Jolly Jingles for the Jewish Child* ©1947; "S'vivon" by L. Kipnis, "Mo'oz Tsur" English verse by M. Jastrow, "Oh Hanuka" versions by M. Riverman, E. Indelman, and F. Minkoff, "Once an Evil King" by H. Reinstein and H. Coopersmith, "Mi Y'malel" by B.M. Edidin, adapted by M. Ravina, "My Drëdl" by S.S. Grossman and S.E. Goldfarb, and "Shalom Haverim" from *The New Jewish Songbook* by Harry Coopersmith ©1965. Reprinted with the permission of the publisher, Behrman House, Inc.

"Deborah, Woman of Flames" from *Miriam's Well: Rituals for Jewish Women around the Year* by Penina V. Adelman, 2nd ed. ©1990 Biblio Press, NY. (This selection is from an oral *midrash* presented by Janet Zimmerman-Kahan in 1983.)

"The Tear of Repentance: A Yom Kippur Fantasy" by Dorothy Zeligs from *The Story of Jewish Holidays and Customs for Young People* ©1942; "The New Year" and "The Tale of Hanukkah Retold by This Gay Minstrel's Pen of Gold" by Abraham Burstein from *A Jewish Child's Garden of Verse* ©1940; "The Jewish Year" by Jessie Sampter from *Around the Year in Rhymes for the Jewish Child* ©1920; "Hanukkah Lights" from *The Collected Poems of Phillip Raskin: 1878–1944* ©1951. "One Hanukkah in Helm" by Yaacov Luria from *More World over Stories, Vol. 5* ©1960. All reprinted with permission of Bloch Publishing Company.

"In the Days of Awe" by Ruth F. Brin from *A Rag of Love* ©1969. Emmett Publishing. Reprinted by permission of the author.

"New Blessing for Hanukah Candlelighting" by Marcia Lee Falk ©2006. Adapted by the author from a blessing in her book *The Book of Blessings: New Jewish Prayers for Daily Life, the Sabbath, and the New Moon Festival* (Harper 1996; paperback, Beacon Press 1999). Reprinted by permission of the author.

"The Announcing Tool" reprinted by permission of the author, Rabbi Marc Gellman, PhD. Gellman is the author of many children's books, including *Does God Have a Big Toe?*

"Like the Clay in the Hand of the Potter," traditional prayer from *High Holy Day Prayer Book*, p. 538, translated and edited by Philip Birnbaum. Reprinted by permission of the Hebrew Publishing Company.

"Chanukah/Solstice" by Linda Hirschhorn from her *Gather Round* CD ©1989. Reprinted by permission of the author. More of her music can be found at www.lindahirschhorn.com.

"The Never-Ending Song" by Nina Jaffe from *The Uninvited Guest and Other Jewish Holiday Tales* ©1993. Reprinted by permission of the author.

"How to Sell a Menorah," "A Secret Chanukah," and "How Chanukah Came to Be" from *Eight Tales for Eight Nights* by Peninnah Schram, Steven M. Rosman and Tsirl Waletzky ©1990. Reprinted by permission of the publisher, Jason Aronson, Inc.

"Happy Birthday World" by Sadie Rose Weilerstein from *What the Moon Brought* ©1942; "Repentant Jews" from *The Rosh Hashanah Anthology* ©1970; "See, the Conqu'ring Hero Comes" by George F. Handel; "Hanukkah" by Levin Kipnis from *The Hanukkah Anthology* ©1976. All used by permission of the Jewish Publication Society of America.

"Sounding an Alarm: A Rosh Hashanah Parable," Tapuchim Ud'Vash: Apples and Honey," "L'Shanah Tovah," and "Blessing Translation" from *My Very Own Rosh Hashanah Book* by Judyth Robbins Saypol ©1978; "Chag Ha-Or" from *My Very Own Chanukah Book* by Judyth Robbins Saypol ©1977; "I Like Latkes" and "Mind Teaser" by David Adler from *Jewish Holiday Fun* ©1987. Published by Kar-Ben Copies, Inc., Rockville, MD. Used by permission.

"Bee-utiful Candles" by Leonard Jaffe from *The Pitzel Holiday Book* ©1962. Used by permission Ktav Publishing House.

"Maybe Even Higher" by I.L. Peretz from *The Family Treasury of Jewish Holidays* by Malka Drucker ©1994. Reprinted by permission of Little, Brown, and Company.

"Who Can Despise a People with Women Like This?" David Rosenberg's version of "The Book of Judith" has been published in *A Blazing Fountain* (Schocken 1978), *Chosen Days: Celebrating Jewish Festivals in Poetry and Art* (Doubleday 1980), and *A Poet's Bible* (Hyperion 1991) ©1978, 1980, 1991 and 1997 by David Rosenberg. Reprinted by permission of the author.

"Vahakimoti Et B'riti" by Rabbi Moshe Rothblum from *Sounds of Creation: Genesis in Song* ©1992. Reprinted by permission of the author.

"Sound of the Trumpet" by Fania Kruger from *The Tenth Jew* ©1949. Reprinted by permission of Sid Smith.

"Chanukah" recorder duet from Gerald and Sonya Burkoff's *Let's Play* ©1986. Reprinted by permission of Sweet Pipes Music.

"Yotzer Or" and "Chasidic Tale" by Joel Lurie Grishaver from *Building Jewish Life: Rosh Ha-Shanah and Yom Kippur* ©1987; "A Teaching by Rabbi Avi Weiss" and excerpt from "Vataher Libenu" by Rabbi Kerry M. Olitzky from *Eight Nights, Eight Lights* ©1994. Reprinted by permission of Torah Aura Productions.

"The Shofar's Sound," "Rosh Hashanah Is Here," "Spin, Little Dreidels," "Nine Little Candles," "Five Little Latkes in the Frying Pan," and "So Many Candles" by Sylvia Rouss from *Fun with Jewish Holiday Rhymes* ©1992; "Eight Are the Lights" by Ilo Orleans from *Within Thy Hand: My Poem Book of Prayers* ©1961. Reprinted by permission of the Union of American Hebrew Congregations Press.

"Light One Candle," lyrics by Peter Yarrow ©1983. Silver Dawn Music ASCAP. Reprinted by permission of the author.

"It Happened on Hanukkah" by Nathan Alterman, translated by Steve Friedman from *The Young Judean 49, No. 30* ©1960. Reprinted by permission of The Young Judean Hadassah Zionist Youth Commission.

All attempts to locate the following sources for copyright permission have been unsuccessful, and the author would appreciate any information that would provide contact.

"A Hanukkah Top" by Nahum Karpivner from *Gems of Hebrew Verse: Poems for Young People*, Bruce Humphries, 1940.

"Dona Gracia Nasi Mendes: An Ethical Will," author unknown, and "An Unusual Diary Entry" by Menachem Mendel from *Jews of the Sepharad,* Coalition for the Advancement of Jewish Education (CAJE) Publications, 1991.

"A Syrian Diary" by Joseph Hapern from *Storytime: A Jewish Children's Story-Book,* Edward Goldstone Publishers, 1946.

"For a Good and a Sweet New Year" by Sadie Rose Weilerstein from *The Singing Way: Poems for Jewish Children*, and "Dreidel Song" by Efraim Rosenzweig from *More Poetry for the Holidays*, Garrard Publishing, 1973.

"The Seven Brothers and Their Mother" by Solomon Zeitlin from *The Second Book of Maccabees,* Harper and Brothers for Dropsie College for Hebrew and Cognate Learning, 1954.

"The Legend of the Jewish Pope" by Micha Bin Gorion from *Popes from the Ghetto: A View of Medieval Christendom*, Horizon Press, 1966.

"Ocho Kandelikas" by Flory Jagoda from *Kantikas Di Mi Nona*, Global Village, 1996.

"My Dreidel" by Hayyim Nahman Bialik from *Jewish Life and Customs, Unit Four: Hanukkah*, Jewish Education Committee, 1942.

"Rosh Hashanah Eve" by Harry Phillip in *Poems for Jewish Holidays* by Myra Cohn Livingston, ed., Holiday House, 1986.

"Kindle the Taper" by Emma Lazarus.

"A Sweet New Year" by Levin Kipnis from *My Holidays: Holiday Stories for Children*, Tversky Publication House, Tel Aviv, 1961.

"Selichot Prayers" by David De Sola Pool, ed., from *Prayers for the New Year According to the Custom of the Spanish and Portuguese Jews*, Union of Sephardic Congregations, NY, 1960.

Endnotes

1 Almon, Joan. "Cultural Diversity and the Universal Human," in *Multiculturalism in Waldorf Education,* No. 3. Fair Oaks, CA: AWSNA Publications, 1993, p 1.

2 Ibid.

3 Spiegel, Marcia Cohen. *Women in the Bible*: *Study Course.* New York: Women's League for Conservative Judaism, no date, pp 39–41.

4 Jaffe, Nina. *The Uninvited Guest and Other Jewish Holiday Tales.* New York: Scholastic Inc., 1993, p 62.

5 Ibid.

6 Steiner, Rudolf. *Study of Man.* Translated by A.C. Harwood, London: Rudolf Steiner Press, 2004, p 190.

7 Due to the nature of the Jewish calendar, every three or four years Rosh Hashanah may occur during the last week of September or the first days of October.

8 Waskow, Arthur Ocean. *Seasons of Our Joy.* Boston: Beacon Press, 1982, p 5.

9 *Erev* is the word used to signify the eve before a holy day. Because the Jewish day begins at sundown, there are shorter Erev services 'the night before,' which continue in the morning on the following day. For Jewish people they are considered part of the same day.

10 Grishaver, Joel Lurie, ed. *Building Jewish Life: Rosh Ha-Shanah and Yom Kippur.* Los Angeles: Torah Aura Productions, 1987, p 42.

11 Rabbi Areyeh Hirschfield, Kol Nidre Service, 1996.

12 Ibid.

13 Steiner, Rudolf. *The Archangel Michael: His Mission and Ours.* Translated by Marjorie Spock, New York: Anthroposophic Press, 1994, p 65.

14 Ibid., pp 91, 94.

15 Ibid., pp 95–96.

16 Goodman, Philip, ed. *The Rosh Hashanah Anthology.* Philadelphia: The Jewish Publication Society of America, 1970, p 240.

17 Fox, Rabbi Karen L. and Phyllis Zimbler Miller. *Seasons for Celebration.* New York: Putnam Publishing Group, 1992, p 41.

18 Strassfeld, Michael. *The Jewish Holidays: A Guide and Commentary.* New York: Harper and Row, 1985, p 98.

19 Op. cit., Wascow, pp 20–21.

20 Falcon, Rabbi Theodore. *Meditations for the High Holy Days.* Woodland Hills, CA: Makom Ohr Shalom, 1987, p 20.

21 Op. cit., Fox, p 42.

22 Saypol, Judyth Robbins and Madeline Wikler. *My Very Own Rosh Hashanah Book.* Rockville, MD: Kar-Ben Copies, Inc., 1978, p 24.

23 Op. cit., Goodman. *Rosh Hashanah Anthology*, p 338.

24 Rouss, Sylvia A. *Fun with Jewish Holiday Rhymes.* New York: Union of American Hebrew Congregations (UAHC) Press, 1992, p 1.

25 Larrick, Nancy, ed. *More Poetry for the Holidays.* Champaign, IL: Garrard Publishing Co., 1973, p 35.

26 Op. cit., Goodman. *Rosh Hashanah Anthology*, pp 306–309.

27 Brinn, Ruth Esrig. *Jewish Holiday Games for Little Hands.* Rockville, MD: Kar-Ben Copies, Inc., 1993.

28 Op. cit., Goodman. *Rosh Hashanah Anthology*, p 337.

29 Op. cit., Larrick, p 34.

30 Drucker, Malka, ed. *The Family Treasury of Jewish Holidays.* New York: Little, Brown and Company, 1994, pp 10–14.

31 Op. cit., Goodman. *Rosh Hashanah Anthology*, pp 350–351.

32 Op. cit., Jaffe, p 9.

33 I highly recommend Clyde Robert Bulla's version in *The Family Treasury of Jewish Holidays,* edited by Malka Drucker, pp 19–24.

34 Op. cit., Strassfeld, p 99.

35 Op. cit., Rouss, p 1.

36 Op. cit., Grishaver, p 27.

37 Op. cit., Goodman. *Rosh Hashanah Anthology*, pp 322–325.

38 In the Jewish Kabbalistic tradition, Michael is the angel on the right, Gabriel is on the left, Raphael is behind, and Uriel is in front. (Explanation of "Dream Pillow" available from Tiferet Studios, P.O. Box 27444, Philadelphia, PA, 1994.)

39 Op. cit., Grishaver, pp 32–37.

40 Ibid., pp 52–54.

41 Ibid., p 79.

42 Livingston, Myra Cohn. *Poems for Jewish Holidays.* New York: Holiday House, 1986, p 6.

43 Op. cit., Jaffe, pp 11–16, 62.

44 Sadker, Myra. *Failing at Fairness: How Our Schools Cheat Girls.* New York: Simon & Schuster, 1995.

45	Op. cit., Goodman. *Rosh Hashanah Anthology*, p 238.
46	Op. cit. Saypol and Wikler, p 17.
47	Op. cit., Goodman. *Rosh Hashanah Anthology*, p 341.
48	Ibid., pp 333–336.
49	Ibid., translated by Joachim Prinz, p 138.
50	De Sola Pool, David, ed. *Prayers for the New Year According to the Custom of the Spanish and Portuguese Jews*. New York: Union of Sephardic Congregations, 1960, pp 91–93.
51	Op. cit., Goodman. *Rosh Hashanah Anthology*, p 340.
52	Behar, Cantor Isaac. *The High Holy Days Pizmonim and Selihot in Ladino*. Los Angeles: Sephardic Temple Tifereth Israel, p 5.
53	Op. cit., De Sola Pool, p 2.
54	Op. cit., Behar, p 6.
55	Op cit., De Sola Pool.
56	Policker, R. Personal conversation, October 11, 1996.
57	Goodman, Philip, ed. *The Yom Kippur Anthology*. Philadelphia: The Jewish Publication Society of America, 1971, p 64.
58	Kordova, Lea-Nora and Annette & Eugene Labovitz, eds. *Our Story, Jews of the Sepharad, Celebrations and Stories*. New York: Coalition for the Advancement of Jewish Education (CAJE) Publications, 1991, pp 18–22.
59	Ibid., pp 42–45.
60	Tisha B'Av is the day in the Hebrew calendar set aside specifically as a day of mourning in remembrance of the destruction of the first Temple, built by King Solomon, as well as other destructive acts inflicted upon the Jews throughout history.
61	Op. cit., Saypol and Wikler, pp 26–27.
62	Ibid., p 31.
63	Ibid., pp 26–27.
64	Reuben, Steve. *Especially Wonderful Days*. Denver: A.R.E. Publishing, 1976.
65	Milgrom, Rabbi Shira. *The Untold Story of Chanukah*, cassette tape recording. New York: The National Jewish Center for Learning and Leadership, 1990.
66	Olitzky, Rabbi Kerry M. *Eight Nights, Eight Lights*. Los Angeles: Alef Design Group, 1994, p 18.
67	Pietzner, Carlos. *Festival Images for Today*. New York: Anthroposophic Press, 1993, pp 75–76.

68   Ibid., p 91.

69   Copy editor for Shabbat Shenit Hanukah Service. Unpublished proceedings from Study Group, December 1994.

70   Goodman, Philip, ed. *The Hannukah Anthology*. Philadelphia: The Jewish Publication Society of America, 1976, p 265.

71   Traditional blessing.

72   Op. cit., Fox, p 95.

73   Traditional blessing.

74   Falk, Marcia. Personal conversation, September 2006.

75   Ibid.

76   An easy approach to making rolled candles is to purchase the honeycomb beeswax available through Mercurius USA, 4321 Anthony Court, Rocklin, CA, info@mercurius-usa.com.

77   Foby, Shannon. Personal conversation, 2006.

78   Op. cit., Larrick, p 46.

79   Op. cit., Rouss, p 10.

80   Ibid., p 11.

81   Ibid., p 12.

82   Op. cit., Goodman. *Hanukkah Anthology*, pp 307–313.

83   Adler, David A. *Jewish Holiday Fun*. Rockville, MD: Kar-Ben Copies, Inc., 1987, p 30.

84   Op. cit., Larrick, p 45.

85   Op. cit., Rouss, p 11.

86   Adelman, Penina. *Miriam's Well: Rituals for Jewish Women around the Year*, 2nd ed. New York: Biblio Press, 1990, pp 37–38.

87   The English translation is: "How good it is for people to come together and live in peace." There is a beautiful round using these words that is frequently sung in third grade classrooms as an opening or closing song for the day.

88   Op. cit., Goodman. *Hanukkah Anthology*, pp 324–328.

89   Ibid., p 396.

90   Op. cit., Olitzky, p 19.

91   Op. cit., Goodman. *Hanukkah Anthology*, pp 373–378.

92   Op. cit., Saypol and Wikler, *Chanukah Book*, p 15.

93 Goodman, Robert. *A Teacher's Guide to Jewish Holidays.* Denver: A.R.E. Publishing, 1983, p 92.

94 Op. cit., Adler, p 28.

95 Op. cit., Goodman. *Hanukkah Anthology,* pp 372–373.

96 Op. cit., Adler, p 34.

97 Schram, Peninnah, Steven M. Rosman and Tsirl Waletzky. *Eight Tales for Eight Nights: Stories for Chanukah.* Northvale, NJ: Jason Aronson, 1990, pp 63–67.

98 Op. cit., Shabbat Shenit Study Group, 1991.

99 Op. cit., Goodman. *Hanukkah Anthology,* p 363.

100 Shabbat Shenit Study Group, December 1992.

101 Rosenberg, David. *Chosen Days: Celebrating Jewish Festivals in Poetry and Art.* New York: Doubleday, 1980, pp 101–115.

102 Yolen, Jane. *Milk and Honey: A Year of Jewish Holidays.* New York: G.P. Putnam's Sons, 1996, p 33.

103 Op. cit., Goodman. *Hanukkah Anthology,* p 36.

104 Ibid., pp 342–347.

105 Ibid., pp 52–55.

106 Op. cit., Kordova, p 15.

107 Ibid., p 18.

108 Ibid., p 7.

109 www.davka.org/what/text/liturgies/Chanukah/Chanukah.15.html. This verse is also available as a choral arrangement through stagepass.com. To hear Ms. Jagoda sing it, go to www.songsforteaching.homestead.com/ChanukahOchoKandelikas.html.

110 Op. cit., Goodman. *Hanukkah Anthology,* pp 367–368.

111 Op. cit., Schram, pp 53–58.

112 Op. cit., Goodman. *Hanukkah Anthology,* pp 369–371.

113 Shabbat Shenit Study Group, 1993. Song tune can be found at www.peterpaul andmary.com/music/14-10.htm, which has listings of albums and sheet music sources.

114 Op. cit., Olitzky, p 19.

115 Op. cit., Schram, pp 5–10.

Bibliography

Adelman, Penina V., ed. *Miriam's Well: Rituals for Jewish Women around the Year.* New York: Biblio Press, 1990.

Adler, David A. *Jewish Holiday Fun.* Rockville, MD: Kar-Ben Copies, Inc., 1987.

Aleichem, Sholem. *Holiday Tales.* trans. Aliza Shevrin, New York: Aladdin, 1979.

Algazi, Leon. *Chants Sephardis.* Paris: Publications De La Federation Sephardite Mondiale Departement Cultural, 1957.

Almon, Joan. "Cultural Diversity and the Universal Human," in *Multiculturalism in Waldorf Education*, No. 3. Fair Oaks, CA: AWSNA Publications, 1993.

Azose, Hazan Isaac and Isaac Maimon. *Agada de Pesah.* Bellevue, WA: M. & M. Piha, 1995.

Behar, Cantor Isaac. *The High Holy Days Pizmonim and Selihot in Ladino.* Los Angeles: Sephardic Temple Tifereth Israel, no date.

Black, Naomi, ed. *Celebration: The Book of Jewish Festivals.* Middle Village, NY: Jonathan David Publishers, 1989.

Brinn, Ruth Esrig. *Jewish Holiday Crafts for Little Hands.* Rockville, MD: Kar-Ben Copies, Inc., 1993.

_____. *Jewish Holiday Games for Little Hands.* Rockville, MD: Kar-Ben Copies, Inc., 1995.

Buell, Ruthie. "The Dreydl Song," on *Chanukah at Home,* compact disc. Cambridge, MA: Rounder Records, 1988.

Burakoff, Gerald and Sonya. *Let's Play – Level 1.* Levittown, NY: Sweet Pipes, 1986.

Capel, Evelyn Francis. *The Christian Year.* Edinburgh: Floris Books, 1967.

Chagall, Bella and Marc. *Burning Lights.* New York: Schocken Books, 1962.

Coopersmith, Harry. *The New Jewish Songbook.* West Orange, NJ: Behrman House, 1965.

De Sola Pool, David, ed. *Prayers for the New Year According to the Custom of the Spanish and Portuguese Jews.* New York: Union of Sephardic Congregations, 1960.

Diamant, Anita and Howard Cooper. *Living a Jewish Life.* New York: Harper Perennial, 1991.

Dimont, Max I. *Jews, God and History.* New York: The New American Library, Inc., 1962.

Drucker, Malka, ed. *The Family Treasury of Jewish Holidays.* New York: Little, Brown and Company, 1994.

Falcon, Rabbi Theodore. *Meditations for the High Holy Days.* Woodland Hills, CA: Makom Ohr Shalom, 1987.

Finser, Torin M. *School as a Journey: The Eight-Year Odyssey of a Waldorf Teacher.* New York: Anthroposophic Press, 1994.

_____. *Research: Creating a Community of Research in Waldorf Schools*. Fair Oaks, CA: AWSNA Publications, 1995.

Fox, Rabbi Karen L. and Phyllis Zimbler Miller. *Seasons for Celebration*. New York: Putnam Publishing Group, 1992.

Friedman, Randee. *Sounds of Creation: Genesis in Song*. San Diego: Sounds Write Productions, Inc., 1992.

Goodman, Philip, ed. *The Hanukkah Anthology*. Philadelphia: The Jewish Publication Society of America, 1976.

_____. *The Rosh Hashanah Anthology*. Philadelphia: The Jewish Publication Society of America, 1970.

_____. *The Yom Kippur Anthology*. Philadelphia: The Jewish Publication Society of America, 1971.

Goodman, Robert. *A Teacher's Guide to Jewish Holidays*. Denver: A.R.E. Publishing, 1983.

Grishaver, Joel Lurie. *Building Jewish Life: Rosh Ha-Shanah and Yom Kippur*. Los Angeles: Torah Aura Productions, 1987.

Hubbard, Ruth Shagoury and Brenda Miller Power. *The Art of Classroom Inquiry: A Handbook for Teacher-Researchers*. Portsmouth, NH: Heinemann, 1993.

Jaffe, Nina. *The Uninvited Guest and Other Jewish Holiday Tales*. New York: Scholastic Inc., 1993.

Kordova, Lea-Nora and Annette & Eugene Labovitz, eds. *Our Story, Jews of the Sepharad, Celebrations and Stories*. New York: Coalition for the Advancement of Jewish Education (CAJE) Publications, 1991.

Larrick, Nancy, ed. *More Poetry for the Holidays*. Champaign, IL: Garrard Publishing Co., 1973.

Levine, Elizabeth Resnick. *A Ceremonies Sampler: New Rites, Celebrations, and Observations of Jewish Women*. San Diego: Women's Institute for Continuing Jewish Education, 1993.

Livingston, Myra Cohn. *Poems for Jewish Holidays*. New York: Holiday House, 19, 1986.

Margolies, Morris B. *A Gathering of Angels: Angels in Jewish Life and Literature*. New York: Ballantine Books, 1994.

Milgrom, Rabbi Shira, speaker. *The Untold Story of Chanukah,* cassette recording. New York: The National Jewish Center for Learning and Leadership, 1990.

Olitzky, Kerry M. *Eight Nights, Eight Lights*. Los Angeles: Alef Design Group, Torah Aura Productions, 1994.

Patterson, José. *Angels, Prophets, Rabbis and Kings from the Stories of the Jewish People*. New York: P. Bedrick Books, 1991.

Pietzner, Carlos. *Festival Images for Today*. New York: Anthroposophic Press, 1993.

Prokofieff, Sergei O. *The Cycle of the Year as a Path of Initiation Leading to an Experience of the Christ Being*. London: Temple Lodge Publishing, 1995.

Reuben, Steve. *Especially Wonderful Days*. Denver: A.R.E. Publishing, 1976.

Rosenberg, David. *Chosen Days: Celebrating Jewish Festivals in Poetry and Art*. New York: Doubleday, 1980.

Rouss, Sylvia A. *Fun with Jewish Holiday Rhymes*. New York: Union of American Hebrew Congregations (UAHC) Press, 1992.

Sadker, Myra. *Failing at Fairness: How Our Schools Cheat Girls*. New York: Simon & Schuster, 1995.

Saypol, Judyth Robbins and Madeline Wikler. *My Very Own Chanukah Book*. Rockville, MD: Kar-Ben Copies, Inc., 1977.

_____. *My Very Own Rosh Hashanah Book*. Rockville, MD: Kar-Ben Copies, Inc., 1978.

_____. *My Very Own Yom Kippur Book*. Rockville, MD: Kar-Ben Copies, Inc., 1978.

Schram, Peninnah, Steven M. Rosman and Tsirl Waletzky. *Eight Tales for Eight Nights: Stories for Chanukah*. Northvale, NJ: Jason Aronson, Inc., 1990.

Schwartz, Eugene. "Some Thoughts on the Chanukah Festival," *Anthroposophic Society Newsletter*.

Shabbat Shenit Hanukah Service, copy editor. Unpublished Proceedings from Study Groups, 1991 and 1993.

Singer, Isaac Bashevis. *Zlateh the Goat and Other Stories*. New York: Harper Collins, 1966.

Spiegel, Marcia Cohen. *Women in the Bible: Study Course*. New York: Women's League for Conservative Judaism, no date.

Steiner, Rudolf. *The Archangel Michael: His Mission and Ours*. trans. Marjorie Spock, New York: Anthroposophic Press, 1994.

_____. *The Cycle of the Year as Breathing-Process of the Earth*. New York: Anthroposophic Press, 1984.

_____. *Discussions with Teachers*. London: Rudolf Steiner Press, 1992.

_____. *Practical Advice to Teachers*. New York: Anthroposophic Press, 1988.

_____. *Study of Man*. trans. A.C. Harwood, London: Rudolf Steiner Press, 2004.

Strassfeld, Michael. *The Jewish Holidays: A Guide and Commentary*. New York: Harper and Row, 1985.

Waskow, Arthur Ocean. *Seasons of Our Joy*. Boston: Beacon Press, 1982.

Yolen, Jane. *Milk and Honey: A Year of Jewish Holidays*. New York: G.P. Putnam's Sons, 1996.